Printed in China

Editor: Mike Barnes. Sub-editor: Jane Pruden
Book design and illustration: Anthony Hall, BPG Media
Chapter 15 illustrations: Rodger McPhail
Cover photograph: Paul Gillis

The Sporting Library
Buckminster Yard
Buckminster
Grantham
Lincolnshire NG33 5SB
Email: info@thesportinglibrary.co.uk
www.thesportinglibrary.co.uk

I started rabbiting in a big way: I had about ten ferrets. By this time, my mother was more relaxed about my country pursuits, but my father thought I ought to be spending more time on my schoolwork. I had started at Frome prep school, and then was sent away to board at Monkton Combe when I was 10. I was never academic, but loved sport right from the start.

I was lucky to be able to play sport at all, as I had a dreadful accident when I was five years old. At breakfast one day, my mother noticed that our chickens – we had Rhode Island Reds – had got out, and were pecking at the lawn, so I went out with my sister, Valerie, to round them up. I then challenged her to race back to the house. I was winning, and turned to see how far behind she was... and then ran straight into the french windows. I saw them just in time, and put both arms out to save myself. I cut open my left wrist, but sliced my right arm from the wrist almost to my shoulder: flaps of flesh were hanging off.

My mother had worked as an army nurse in the First World War, and, afterwards as a sister in the Bristol Royal Infirmary, so she knew what to do. She bandaged me up as best she could to stop the worst of the bleeding, and got me to hospital. They gave me ether, and then put 55 stitches in my right arm. It was nearly a year before I got back full use of it.

Not long after that, I had an accident while riding my sister's horse, called Wings. I slipped off, and my foot caught in the stirrup, and I was dragged along about 100 yards, knocking myself out in the process. I had severe concussion, and also contracted jaundice as a result. I was off school for six weeks.

I was lucky to reach my teens as well. My school-friend Harrison-Smith, who lived in Bath, used to stay with us for a few days during the Christmas holidays, as he was as keen on shooting as I was. One day we went out rabbiting on a farm nearby where there was a brook with withy trees alongside it. The rabbits used to get up into the trees, but I would ferret the holes below. We both had .410s, and as I bent down to put a ferret in, a rabbit bolted down the nearest tree. Harry fired at it... just as I stood up. I was hit in the right side of my face with – thankfully – the edge of the pattern, but got a cheekful of pellets, and my ear was badly peppered. The blood was pouring out.

I can't have been that concerned by it, as I remember that when we were cycling back home – with rabbits dangling from the handlebars, and the ferrets in a box on the back – I saw a covey of partridges huddling together in the snow. This was too good an opportunity to miss, and I loaded the .410, and got six of them with one

At Southfield, aged 10, with the BSA air rifle,
Sally the lab and the first of many Beauts.

shot. One was only winged, and I hared after it, my blood dripping down in the snow along with the partridge's.

Harry was upset, of course. He was worried that his father would get to hear about it, but my immediate concern was what my mother would say when we got home. She said: 'What have you done? I knew this would happen!' and I tried to reassure her that it was just a few pellets, and there was no real harm done.

I had to go to Frome hospital, though, and they dug most of the pellets out of my face. They missed two, though, which I can still feel, underneath my hair. I was lucky: six inches to the left, and I'd have been blinded, if not killed.

We had never been taught safety as such. You often read about boys being carefully supervised while learning to shoot, and having to carry an unloaded gun for a season before they were allowed to fire a cartridge. There was none of that for me: I just learned it as I went along – and so did Harrison-Smith!

I've only had one other near miss. It was when I was hare shooting on Lockinge Estate in Berkshire – we killed over 800 that day, and, afterwards, while we were standing round, chatting, the chap next door to me was cradling a hammer gun, and it just went off! He hadn't unloaded it, and the hammer fell. I felt the charge go past my head: again, six inches to the side, and I'd have been dead.

At Monkton Combe, I was playing hockey, rugby, fives... and, my first love, cricket. I was called 'Fisty' as I had had a bit of a barney with a senior who pushed me in the dining room. He was a prefect, and probably 17, and slapped me on the back of the head, and told me to get in line. I was only 11, but I turned round and floored him. The whole line cheered, but it was all covered up. After that, I joined the boxing team.

I had my front teeth knocked out, during the school diving competition. As I came up from a dive, someone else dived in, and hit me in the face! I had to wear a plate after that. Years later, I was wildfowling with Ray Hillyer and his father, Bob, on the Somerset Levels. I was a bit of a mentor to Ray, who turned into an excellent Shot, and a great countryman. He loves his pigeon shooting, too. It had turned very wet, and only young Ray – he was about 17 then – was enthusiastic enough to come with me, and try for a mallard or two. On our way home, in the gathering gloom, I tried to cross a rhyne, but I misjudged it. As I went in, my plate came out! I stayed there, soaked through, and sent young Ray back to the pub, The Black Smock, to get a torch. It was quite a trip in the dark, but eventually he came back. The water level had dropped a bit... and there were my teeth! I picked up the plate, rinsed it off, and popped it back in! I lost them again one night after a great win against Sherborne at cricket: I'd been celebrating a bit enthusiastically... but that's another story!

Frank Vallis was the groundsman and coach for cricket and rugby at the Senior School. We called him 'Pro'. He came up to me one day, and said: 'Fisty, we've got problems with rabbits on the cricket square. Can you get rid of them?' I told him I'd put some wires down, and that would sort them out. There was an old GWR railway line alongside the cricket field – they filmed *The Titchfield Thunderbolt* there – and the embankment was very overgrown, which is where the rabbits were coming from.

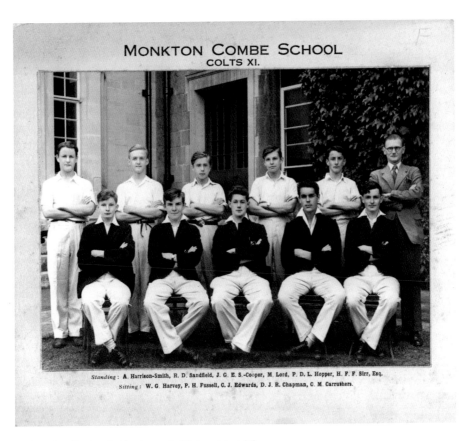

Cricket colts – Harrison-Smith, who nearly killed me, is back left.

My friend Harrison-Smith helped me. We were pretty surreptitious about it, and caught quite a few, which I was going to take home and sell. I'd 'legged' them, and hung them on the handlebars of my bike, which I left under the viaduct. It was after chapel on the last Sunday of the winter term, and I had my school blazer on, when a little inspection truck came down the railway line. The workers on it saw Harry and me riding our bikes out from under the viaduct, and they went and told the headmaster that they had seen boys poaching on railway property.

The headmaster called an assembly, and told the whole school that if the two boys responsible didn't own up, he would keep the entire school in for an extra day, when the holidays started. The whole school seemed to turn and look at Harry and me, so we went direct to the Head, and I explained that I was doing this at the behest of the 'Pro'. He was very understanding, but said that I should have let him know what we were doing first.

My schoolwork suffered from my love of sport, and my school reports were poor. It got to the stage where the headmaster said I would get nowhere by just playing sport, and that unless there was an improvement 'The axe would have to fall!' My father was horrified at the thought of his son being expelled from school, and I promised to do my best to improve. My cricketing ability saved me: though still only a Junior Colt, I was taking a lot of wickets with my leg-breaks, and got into the First XI, just in time for the annual grudge match against King's School, Bruton. We hadn't beaten them for five years, but I managed to take 8 for 22, and we thrashed them. The following day, my housemaster told me the Head wanted to see me, and I feared the worst. Instead, he congratulated me, and said 'The axe won't fall!'

On holiday in Teignmouth in 1946
with sisters Valerie (left) and Barbara.

After the war, I used to spend my holidays with my Uncle Frank on his farm at Minchington, in Dorset, and all my time was taken up, catching, or shooting rabbits, which I'd sell to a black-marketeer, who had a pub in the village. He'd take pigeons and any game I could get, too. I'd write down on a bit of paper how many rabbits I'd given him. He was a crafty one, though, and he'd always knock a bit off for rabbits that were badly shot. I was about 15 then, and making good money, as rabbits fetched a shilling each.

My uncle had an old 12 bore hammer gun, which would only go off in one barrel. He'd get me the cartridges, but I had to be careful with them. There was a hill on the farm, called Hungry Hill, with a lot of sour grass on it, but it was covered in rabbits. Every tussock would have a rabbit in it, sometimes two. If there were two, I'd shoot them in the tussock with one shot; if only one, Uncle would tap it out, and I'd shoot it running. I couldn't get two running, because of the faulty barrel.

If I ran out of cartridges, I'd go and put my hat on a stick, in front of the squat, and I'd then creep round behind. The rabbits would watch the stick with the hat on, and I could sneak up behind them, and catch them in my hands.

I'd also go with an old keeper, Ted Broadway – and his friend Ben Crees – and we'd ferret the rabbits, and, when we had ten, he would stick one in the ferret box, and when I was ready, he'd open the door. Out would hop the rabbit, and just sit there for a minute, sizing up his surroundings, and then he'd make a bolt for it, and I'd have a go with my .410. If I missed, I could see where the shot had gone in the grass, and the old boy would say: 'You were behind 'ee.' I wasn't allowed too many shots, as you didn't get as much for a shot rabbit as a trapped one. I got so good at it, that I rarely missed.

When I left school, I was already marked down as working on the farm, so I was exempt from National Service. I wanted to learn more about farming, and I went to work – for no wages – on Norton Tilley's Bridge Farm, at Britford-on-Avon, near Salisbury. My mother used to send me a postal order for 12s/6d every week, and I supplemented that with a bit of poaching here and there, and selling rabbits. Most of it went on beer, as I'd now discovered drinking.

I joined Salisbury Young Farmers, and met a fair few young ladies, who all seemed to develop an interest in seeing the poultry pens, which I looked after, in the farm water-meadows. I've got fond memories of those water-meadows!

Fussells owned the Cathedral Hotel in Salisbury, which was run by our manager, Alan Hinman. I'd either drop off rabbits to him, or get them delivered with his beer, by one of our lorries, if I'd got a few when I was home at weekends. He paid me in cash, so it wasn't going through the books, but my father got to hear about this, and worked out that Mr Hinman was making a bit on the side, and he was sacked. I then had to find a new outlet for my wares, but it was mostly local butchers, and they didn't pay nearly so well.

While at Bridge Farm, I met Lord Porchester, who, at that time, was the Queen's racehorse trainer. The farm bordered the Christie-Miller's Clarendon estate, on one side, and Lord Radnor's, too. All these estates got together on August 12th, and shot the ducks off the Avon. On Lord Radnor's land there was a bridge across the river, where they used to string a net to catch any of the dead ducks floating downstream. No dogs were allowed to pick up during the shoot, in case they scared the ducks off.

The ducks would go stubbling at dusk, and through the night, and come back during the morning. I'd been asked by Norton Tilley to make three duck hides – for Lord Porchester, Douglas Pilkington and Major Dowling who had the shooting on Bridge Farm. I could hardly wait for the 12th, because there were thousands of ducks. I stood with Lord Porchester, who was about 40 at the time. He shot very well, and then said: 'Young man, do you shoot?', so I replied 'Yes sir!' and he asked me if I'd like to have a shot. He was using a beautiful Purdey, which he lent me, and as soon as I'd taken it from him, two mallard came over, and I knocked them both down stone dead, right and left! He said: 'You've done this before!' He was a real gent. The bag was over 500 that morning – all wild mallard – over the three estates.

The arrival of myxomatosis was a disaster for me. Catching rabbits was my livelihood, really. The farmers were thrilled initially, as rabbits caused so much damage. Some of the downland farms were rent-free, as the crops were so badly hit. It was awful to see the poor rabbits just sitting beside the road, and in the road, just dying, and, of course nobody then wanted to eat them. They had been the staple meat diet of country people. My mother used to cook the livers in beef dripping – they were delicious. I once served them up for George Digweed for breakfast, before we went pigeon shooting. He was very dubious about them, but eventually agreed how good they were. He'd never eaten them before.

The other meal I remember was after the rook shoots. The local squire, Captain Batten-Pool, used to allow the tenants to shoot the rooks early in May, when the young ones were big enough to be hopping round on the branches close to their nests. We'd get hundreds, and my mother would make potted rook, with ham, the young rook breasts and boiled eggs, rather like brawn. She'd turn it out of the bowl, and cut slices, and we'd eat it cold.

With no rabbits to catch, I had to find alternative sources of income: I caught hundreds of moles, and sold the skins. In the spring, after a field had been drilled and rolled, it was easy to see where a mole was working: it would raise the earth a little as it moved under the surface. I'd stamp the earth down about six inches behind it, which would collapse the run, and it was trapped. I'd just put my fingers in, and pull out the mole, and knock it on the head. Then I'd skin them, pin them onto a board to keep the skins flat, and rub them with saltpetre to dry them. My mother complained about the smell! I sold them in 20s to Horace Friend in Lincolnshire – he paid 3d a skin, and I was his best supplier. He took starling and jay wings, and mallard tail feathers too. I used to get some handy cheques back, too: I had a Post Office account which paid 2½% interest, and when you got up to £500, that was the limit! I didn't get any pocket money from my parents, but I made quite a bit on the side from my various activities.

I also turned to more serious poaching. I always had a rifle in the car, and, while on my travels, if I saw a pheasant, I'd pot it from the car window, and pick it up in the dark, later on. Pheasants fetched an amazing price then, compared to today, and I never got caught.

There were always opportunities to make money. A local man, Pat Mitchard, wanted to train his greyhounds, and needed a live rabbit for them to chase, and, hopefully, kill. He asked me if I could get him one, which was no easy task, as there were so few about after myxy had struck. I ferreted about 50 holes before I finally managed to catch one, which I put in an old potato sack. I told Pat I wanted £5 for it, as it had been such a job to catch it, and reluctantly he accepted. We met in the local pub, and I had the rabbit in my old van. When I went to pick up the sack, the rabbit wriggled, and the sack burst at the bottom, where it had been damp, and had gone rotten. The rabbit leapt out of the van, ran down the road and disappeared into someone's garden, with us in hot pursuit. Pat never got his rabbit, and I didn't get my fiver.

In 1955, a local man who had seen me shoot 100 straight in a local Down-the-Line competition, asked me if I'd go down to Monte Carlo, and take part in the live pigeon shooting there. He said he'd sponsor me, and lend me a gun. I was just about to go off with some mates to Spain, but I persuaded them that this year we ought to try Monte. The gun didn't fit me that well, but I did all right, as I was a quick shooter, though I didn't get to the finals, so my sponsor didn't make any money out of me. The rock pigeons came out of holes about 25 yards up in the cliff face – you didn't know which hole they were coming out of – and headed for home, which was a loft, about a mile away. After the second or third round, the trappers would pull a few feathers, to make the birds' flight more erratic, and they were much more difficult to kill.

You had to drop them within a circle; if they died outside the circle they didn't count. It wasn't that difficult, but there was a knack to it: you had to have the gun ready in your shoulder, and shoot fast when you saw the bird. It was easy to see the Guns who had plenty of experience at it: they all took them well out in front, as soon as they saw them.

Monte was rather more expensive than our trips to Spain, and we didn't have much money left. On our last evening, we were in a bar where the barmaid was an absolute cracker. There was a tradition in this bar that you threw a mat with your name on one side, and glue on the other, and tried to stick it on the ceiling. I managed this, and the barmaid told me that if we went down to the casino I should put money on number 32 coming up on the roulette wheel. We were virtually spent out, but I scraped together what was left, and put it on 32. It came up! That paid for us to come home in style.

BBC Radio Bristol asked if they could send James Thorburn out to interview me while I was pigeon shooting, for their farming programme. They would pay me

With my father's Warrilow 12 bore,
and another Beaut carrying an English partridge

15 guineas, and 7½ guineas for each time they repeated the radio interview. James was in the hide with me, and the wires from his mic ran to a van they had to park only about 100 yards away. I had to get them to move it further away – and then it got stuck. It was on a small field of beans, belonging to Alf Paget, near Keynsham. There were stacks of beans left on top, and the field was grey with pigeons, which had mostly come out from Bristol.

Despite all the messing around, I managed to shoot about 170 while we chatted. He'd say: 'Here comes another one – bang – and it's dead!' I'm not sure how well it came across on radio, but I did well, as they broadcast it twice. I got some friends to ring the local BBC and say they'd like to hear it yet again, hoping for more money, but it was never repeated.

About three years ago, I had another visit from the BBC, but this time for television, and I had a couple of very pretty girls in the hide with me. They were very keen on Crumpet, my current springer, and I was very keen on them! I had to be at a pub on top of the Mendips, at five o'clock in the morning, to shoot a field of rape at first light.

The shooting was organised by a pigeon guide, whose name I forget, and I went down to see what was happening the day before. He'd made a hide about the size of a hotel room, with overhead cover as well. I said that I hated being covered over, as I shot a lot of birds directly overhead, but he said that there would be two or three others in the hide with me.

The pigeons came, as I could have predicted, in a mass together. I killed 14 in about 10 minutes, and then it stopped. I wounded one, and it was walking away, so I sent Crumpet to retrieve it. These girls were enchanted with Crumpet's performance, even when I despatched the wounded bird, by wringing its neck. They were asking me all sorts of questions, pointing a thing like a squirrel's tail at me, to record my pearls of wisdom.

After a pause, they asked me if we would stop there all day, and I jokingly replied that they'd be in trouble if they did! I also told them that there would be no more pigeons along for hours, so we might as well pack up. It was quite fun, but I never got paid! I assumed that they'd pay me something, but I was too proud to ask them for anything. Everyone asked how much I'd got paid, and never believed me when I said I'd got nothing – they assumed I'd been paid a lot, and was keeping it secret.

CHAPTER 3

WHAT BETTER BIRD IS THERE TO SHOOT THAN THE WOODPIGEON?

In the 50s and 60s, people who shot game round here – the farmers – finished at the end of January, and never shot the pigeons. They would ring me up and say: 'You've got to come and shoot the pigeons!' I used to shoot a lot at David Taylor's farm at Pimperne, near Blandford. He had asked me to join his pheasant syndicate, but I said that I couldn't possibly afford it. He said not to worry about the money; if I'd shoot the pigeons for him, in return I could have a gun in the shoot!

A lot of rape was grown for the sheep then – rather as stubble turnips sometimes are today – and the woodies would be there in their thousands. It was nothing to shoot 200 or 300. They would just keep decoying. Most often, I would just go up to Great Ridge (a 3,000 acre wood above Fonthill Estate, between Shaftesbury and Warminster), and get my binoculars out, and just watch where the pigeons were flighting to. I'd go there, and set up, and think nothing of shooting 100 in a few hours.

Now, with the shooting pressure, they tend to move around in bigger flocks, so it's more difficult to make a bag. They weren't harassed as they are now, and they decoyed so much more easily. Then, they were a pest, and were shot all the year round. I don't think they are so much, now; I think of them as a gamebird, and don't think they should be shot in the summer. You wouldn't shoot a pheasant or partridge on its nest, so why a pigeon?

Having said that, I sometimes have to go, when a farmer calls, and says someone's got to help him out. If you don't go, you could lose the shooting to someone else. I had to do that last

The legendary Archie Coats

summer: it was early August, and I checked the sex of the birds I shot. Ninety per cent of them were males, which made me feel better, but I still had a guilty conscience. I killed 110 pigeons for 160 shots; and also fired over 200 shells at corvids, and I didn't miss many of them. Not bad at the age of 83! It's a farm where I usually don't like shooting, as the horseflies there are a real menace. On this particular day, though, there were hundreds of swallows swooping about, right up in front of my hide, and I wasn't bothered by any flies at all.

I only met Archie Coats once: he was a professional pigeon shooter, who made his living from it. I was shooting just north of Finkley on a belt, and doing quite well. I saw someone draw up in an old Volvo car, and start watching me, for a long time, and, when I started to pack up – having shot 280 – he came over and chatted to me, saying that he had most of the pigeon shooting in the area, but he could see that I'd done a bit myself! He'd been a Major in the army, and, though I saw him occasionally at game fairs, we were from very different backgrounds, and I didn't go and talk to him again.

Another pigeon guide I knew, was a cricketing friend, Peter Osborne: he did a bit round here. Fred Cooper, Peter and I were the only pigeon shooters in this area. You never saw anyone else. Nowadays, there's so much pressure on the birds. They're getting shot everywhere. Phil Beasley used to guide too, before he brought out the Pigeon Magnet. He was a market trader in the early days, and in the

'A-team'. I remember him phoning me up early one morning from Finmere, near Buckingham, where he was setting up his stall, and telling me there was a hell of a flightline over the market into the neighbouring field. He asked if I could get up there, and I decided to give it a go in my old Subaru. I set off quickly, before I realised I hadn't put in any extra cartridges in the car, and I only had 125. He met me at the gate to the field, and there were pigeons everywhere. There was a little pond on the far side of the field, and I set up there.

I shot hard until it went quiet, and when Phil came to see how I'd got on, I had one shell left. My poor dog retrieved several from the stinky pond, and was covered in black slime. We picked 101 pigeons for those 124 shots, so I'd done quite well! I saw Phil at the CLA Game Fair recently, and one of the first things he said to me was: 'Remember Finmere?'

What chance, though, has a young person got today: someone like me, who started from nothing? These guides charge I don't know how much for pigeon shooting. And the people who come: they turn up in a Range Rover, and start shooting. Most of them don't know the meaning of the word fieldcraft. If you told them to stand on top of a hayrick, they'd do it!

One of the big differences in my heyday was that there was no maize grown. Now, it's everywhere, and you can have some great sport on it when it's been cut in the spring. Then, we used to shoot on beans, and peas, and the spring corn drillings. In the autumn there was beechmast and acorns, and fields of clover. Through the

'Come to my decoys...'

Woodies in flight – a truly sporting bird

winter, the pigeons' diet was largely rape or kale, and when the first drillings went in, they were desperate for it. The drills weren't so good then, and the seed wasn't dressed, so there would be lots of corn on the surface. Now, there's often nothing on top.

It also took a lot longer. Nowadays, with modern machinery, it all goes in very quickly, but then they were often still drilling at the end of April. I never had to travel very far to shoot a decent bag, and I'd have farmers ringing me up, desperate for me to go to their farm the next day.

Then, I used to shoot them all the year round. I used to shoot good bags on hay fields, when the cut grass was full of cocksfoot seeds. The pigeons loved them. They will eat almost anything, though. Ken Raines – an old farming friend, great game and clay Shot, whose favourite saying was: 'The only thing better than pigeon shooting you don't need your trousers for!' – rang me one day and said he'd seen a lot of pigeons near the gallops at Lambourn. He said he couldn't go for a week, but that I should try in the meantime. He said it was stubble, but he wasn't sure why they were on that field. I got set up, and shot well over 200. I couldn't see what they were feeding on, so I opened up several crops, and inside were old, blackened wild oats. I've never seen that since.

When Ken was in hospital after a hip operation, he wanted to make sure his pigeon shooting area in the Cotswolds was covered, so he rang me, and told me where I could find some shooting. Afterwards, another chap who he shot with, contacted him, and said: 'I don't mind you sending someone else up here, but not the best man in the world at it!'

Of course, when there's a big crop of acorns or beechmast, you don't see a pigeon out of the woods until the following spring. If I shoot one during a pheasant or partridge drive, I'll always check its crop. I did the other day: I knew what would be in it: beech nuts – they were packed. Not acorns, as we were on the Downs.

When I was shooting a lot of pigeons, I'd quite often shoot one on the ground, and then another as they flew off. Now, I'm a bit soft: if one lands without me seeing it, I'll shout at it to give it a sporting chance as it flies off. Sometimes, I used to shout at a single pigeon coming into the decoys. They are quite difficult to shoot in that last few yards, when they are looking for a place to land, and dropping a wing to change their flight path. When you shout, they flare away, and make for an easier shot. There's a time and a place to kill an incoming pigeon, and that knowledge only comes with experience. Watch the bird, and how it flies.

I've always shot pigeons sitting down – originally by choice; now because my knees have gone. I can see the bird a long way out, and, from experience, I can read how it is approaching on the wind, and where it is likely to be when I want to take my shot. I then adjust my position on my seat, so that my body angle is right for the shot. It's just as important as getting your feet and body right for any driven bird.

I now use a net and poles, but in the old days, I'd use whatever natural material was available. It was easy to make a hide in a hedge, because they weren't flailed back every year as they are now, or I'd sometimes just hide behind a patch of stinging nettles. I'd want to get going, so I'd make a hide as quickly as possible, and start shooting. Often I'd start with no decoys, or just one or two; that would be enough in those days to attract some more, if you were in the right place, and I usually was. The birds weren't so wary then; now, you must keep hidden, and still, or they will flare away. They

At the end of a day with Phil Beasley, another big bag of woodpigeon

are a different bird today: they used to give themselves up, years ago. In those days, over decoys, I didn't miss many.

My best ever day was March 9th, 1968 at Bill Crouch's Church Farm, near Teffont: I killed 495. I started at first light, and there were so many birds that it soon became clear I was going to run out of cartridges. I usually had three cases of 250 in the car, but that day, I only had two, and a few more in my bag. They were coming beautifully; the wind was just right…and at 2.30 I ran out. I had to drive into Salisbury, pick up another case of cartridges, and I managed about another 25 when I got back in the hide. I lost over an hour of prime time, without which I reckon I'd have killed getting on for 700. I killed 237 on the same field a week later.

As I picked up, on the big day, I saw two foxes, which were 'knotted' at the time, like dogs. Of course, they couldn't get away, and I was able to kill both of them. They were in the next field to where I'd been shooting, so they weren't bothered by it. I dragged them both down to the farmhouse, because I knew Bill would be please to see my success, as he'd been losing a lot of lambs to these foxes, and he said he'd give me a bottle of whisky if I killed one.

So I knocked on the door, and he came out, and said: 'How did you get on, young man?', and I replied: 'Well, Mr. Crouch, I couldn't drive the van down here, and bring the foxes, but I've killed nearly 500 pigeons.' He was thrilled to have got rid of some of the local pigeons, but even more excited about the two foxes – and I got my bottle of whisky as a reward. My old Renault van was filled to the roof that day, and they kept falling onto the front seat on top of my poor tired dog.

I never shot 400 again. I had lots of days in the 300s, but never beat that 495. I used to sell all my

The Pigeon Magnet

pigeons then, to a chap who came down every week from Kent. He took them in the feather. Later on – when I wasn't shooting quite so many – I'd pluck and dress them myself: Bennett's, the butcher in Bath, used to take 150 a week. I've done thousands of pigeons. Even up till quite recently, if I had nothing else to do, I still prepared them. I cut off the head, wings, and feet; stick them in a bucket of water to get the feathers wet; strip them with a plucking machine; gut them, and then rinse them in water, and leave them to dry overnight, before bagging them up. It didn't take long.

Nowadays, some people don't even bother to pick them up. They don't have a dog, and they just leave the dead birds. I've had words with several people about it: it's a travesty. They even leave them in the hide, to rot. Unfortunately, that's the unpleasant face of modern shooting. If you're shooting laid corn, you should try and set up on bare ground nearby, and shoot them there, where you can pick them up. You should always have a dog so that you don't leave wounded birds. A lot of the fun of shooting is working a dog, and they can save you miles of chasing after hit birds.

To show how important I thought it was, always to pick up your birds: one day, I was having a very good shoot on the edge of a wood near Chilmark, by a silage pit. They were flighting in beautifully, and I knew I'd got well over 300, when I saw a line of men walking across the field towards me. I thought I'd better see what they wanted, and realised it was men from Rode village, together with John Steeds, who told me my house was on fire, and that my wife had sent them to find me, as she knew the farm I was shooting on! I asked if the fire brigade was there, and, being told that they were, I said that I'd only go back when I'd picked up my birds. As the eventual pick-up was 370, it took a bit of time, but there was little else I could do, if the fire brigade had it under control!

I've reared pigeons in the past. My spaniel caught one as a squab. It only had one eye, so we called it 'Nelson'. It was two or three months old, and my Jane would rattle a tin, and it would come down to feed. It had a bowl of water, and that bird would wash itself in that water, just like a broody hen.

It got a mate, and this bird would sit up in a tree, about 100 yards away, and you could see it looking, but it would never come down. But then, after about six months, Nelson disappeared: I think a sparrowhawk got it.

I still can't tell the difference between a cock and hen woodpigeon in the feather. When they're plucked, it's a different matter. The best things to eat are a male pigeon's balls! There are two white testicles on its back, and if you pull them out, and fry them in a bit of dripping – delicious! If you have 20 of them: wow – they're a good aphrodisiac, too!

Nowadays of course, there's the Pigeon Magnet. I've never seen the need for them: if I'm in the right place, the pigeons will come. I think it's a lazy man's gadget, eliminating the need for fieldcraft. I remember when Phil Beasley brought it out: he told me that I should have one, and I said I didn't need it. He said I could have one for half price, and that still didn't tempt me. Eventually he sent me one – free – and I still didn't use it. Then, one day, George [Digweed] asked me shooting up in Kent, and he set me up with not one, but three, whirlies going. My poor dog was mesmerised! I shot over 200 pigeons that day, but I told George I reckoned I'd have done just as well without any mechanical assistance.

Of course, movement does attract pigeons: Archie Coats used to throw a bird from the hide into the decoy pattern, and I like floating decoys, bobbing in the wind. I've also used flappers, which can be quite effective. In my youth, if I wingtipped a bird, I'd tie a string from its leg onto a peg. It would walk around in the decoys, and occasionally flap: it was very effective, but, looking back, not too fair on the bird.

I have to admit, though, that I've recently shared a hide with my co-author, Rupert, and he'll use a whirly. I've now seen them pull birds off a distant flightline, so perhaps there's something to them after all. I'm just too lazy to bother setting them up: I'd rather get shooting straight away.

The most satisfying shot is at a high downwind pigeon. I'll always have a go at one, if it's within shot. Timing is everything, as a pigeon can change course with the flick of a wing. A gamebird – once it's on its way – can't manoeuvre like a pigeon. Rock pigeons are protected now, but in the past I shot them, and they can jink more than a woodpigeon. They carry a lot of shot, too. They were the best eating, as they only eat seeds, never green stuff.

Pigeon shooting is for loners really. I'm a loner, but a sociable one! I've always loved pigeon shooting, but equally I love the social side of game shooting, and the lifelong friends I've made through it.

CHAPTER 4

MY MENTORS

Nelson Dance was a key figure in my early years. He was 20 years older than me, and became a bit of a surrogate father, I suppose. He was always very kind: when I was working on the farm near Salisbury, I used to go to a clay pigeon shoot at Hedge End Farm, near Blandford, on a Saturday. I'd get the bus to Blandford, but I had to walk a couple of miles from there, and he would always stop and give me a lift in his Bentley. He'd ask if I had enough cartridges, and I'd say I had a box, as I used to get 25 from Conyer's, the Blandford gunshop, and he'd say: 'Help yourself from my bag', and make sure I filled my pockets.

I'd have a go at the clays, when the competition had finished, as I was still using my uncle's old 12 bore – the one which only worked in one barrel. Old man Browning, who owned Hedge End then, told me to get my father to buy me a better gun! I told him that my father would be mad if he knew I was there, wasting my time, and money, on clay pigeon shooting.

Nelson had shot clays for England, and loved his shooting. He owned Finkley – 1,300 acres to the East of Andover – and had a pheasant shoot there, along

with some wonderful grey partridge ground. The first time I was invited to shoot pheasants, I took the Sauer 12 bore I was then using, with full choke in both barrels. In those days, we used to shoot everything, and a cock pheasant came towards me, only about 15 feet up! I caught it right in the middle, and it just exploded.

At the end of the day, Nelson asked me if I'd enjoyed myself, and, on being told that I'd had a marvellous day, he said: 'Well, you'd better have a brace of birds.' I was handed my brace – a lovely hen, and the smashed-up cock tied alongside it! I never thought I'd get invited again, but he obviously liked me, as he asked me almost every time he shot there.

One summer – it would have been about 1950 – he told me that the Dorset Down-the-Line competition was on at Verwood, and he insisted that I should take part. I wasn't keen, for two reasons: I found Down-the-Line rather boring and repetitive, but, more importantly, the date clashed with an important cricket match between Frome and Blandford.

But he insisted I take part, so I went off early to Verwood, and I knew Cliff Thorne, the man who ran it, and asked if I could have a go, as I had to be away in time for the start of the game at 2.30. He allowed me to enter before the official start time, and to shoot the 100 clays straight off (you usually had four lots of 25), but told me that my score wouldn't count for the prize money, which was about £15 – quite a lot for me, then. I agreed to that, because at least I would have taken part, as Nelson had wanted me to. I shot 99 out of 100! Then Cliff said that seeing how I'd shot 99, he would enter the score.

As I was leaving for cricket, Nelson was driving in, and I said I'd been on already, and I bet him £1 that I'd beat his score. I took six wickets in the match, which we won, and, avoiding the post-match drinks, I hurried back to the shoot, to see if I'd won. As I drove in, Nelson was driving out, carnation still in his buttonhole. He rolled down the window, and said: 'You young bugger! You beat me by one!' and gave me £1 – he'd shot 98. He never forgot it.

After that, he invited me gameshooting, and I had all the pigeon shooting at Finkley for 40 years. He never shot them, but he'd sometimes come and sit in the hide with me, just to watch. Once, he rang me up in the spring, and said: 'You've got to come up: the pigeons are destroying my wheat!' I couldn't understand this, as I'd never heard of pigeons eating growing wheat in the springtime, but, when I drove up to the field, it was grey with woodies. I then saw that the wheat had been drilled in an old potato field, and the pigeons were gorging on the rotting spuds.

For 20 years I shot
a Boss side-by-side

I must have killed a thousand pigeons on that one field in only three days shooting.

Nelson died aged 93. I'd take him fishing on the Test. He'd always want a drink before we started, and he'd get out these plastic glasses – that he never cleaned – and pour us a gin and tonic. It was always the cheapest gin, and the tonic probably a fortnight old from a big bottle! It was flat and horrible: I'd have a small straight gin, as I just couldn't face the tonic. It's my favourite drink, but it's got to be good gin, and fresh tonic.

Coincidentally, his brother married my sister Valerie, before they moved to Australia.

My other close friend was Fred Cooper. He could hardly have been more different than Nelson. He was the local knackerman, a quiet man, a great pigeon Shot – and he taught me all about poaching. He'd always wear a balaclava, so that his face wouldn't be seen. He used to go round all the farms, and he knew where the pheasants were. He was an excellent Shot, though he didn't shoot at stuff more than about 15 yards away.

When I was about 25, I went up to Holbeach with Fred, because I wanted to shoot a goose. We met up with the famous wildfowler, Mackenzie ('Kenzie') Thorpe, who was known as 'The Wild Goose Man'. Fred said to me that we weren't only going wildfowling, but that they also had a few pheasants up there, too. I said I was more interested in the ducks, but he said we should take the rifle, too! He had a little short-barrelled .22 Cogswell & Harrison.

Kenzie Thorpe,
The Wild Goose Man

When we got to Holbeach, we booked in at the local B&B called Selby House. The local wildfowlers weren't at all helpful, but we got an intro to Kenzie Thorpe. I met up with him, and said that I'd come all the way up from Somerset, as I wanted to shoot a wild goose. He said 'It will cost you.' I asked what it would cost for a flight, and he said £5. I said I couldn't afford that, so he asked what I'd give him. I said that Fred didn't want to come, and I'd give him £2 as long as I could shoot a goose, which he finally agreed to.

At 5.30 the next morning, he picked me up in his old van, and we drove down to a potato field, and he was wearing long leather gloves. He asked me: 'Where are your gloves?' and I replied that I didn't know I needed them. He said I'd never get up the dykes with bare hands, as the sides had been swiped, and what was left had needle-sharp points. I said not to worry, and off we went. He had thigh waders, but I only had ordinary Wellington boots – I was really green where coastal wildfowling was concerned.

He was way ahead of me, hurrying down the dyke, and every so often, I had to try and get my balance by putting my hand down to steady myself. He was right, and my hand was soon bleeding away. It was so cold that the safety catch on my Browning seized up. Luckily at that time I smoked, and I held a match to the safety, and thawed it out.

As soon as it started getting light, he started calling the geese, and sure enough, round they came, and we shot three. 'That's enough.' he said. I was happy as I'd got a greylag. Fred was still in bed when I got back!

The local estate, which ran to the sea wall was owned by the Guinnesses. It was well-keepered, and had lots of wild pheasants. After the tide went out, these pheasants would go out across the mud onto these islands. Fred had a marvellous springer called Major, and we'd wait until about 20 pheasants had flown out, and then Fred would send Major out and he'd flush them. They would come back, not very high, and we'd whack them. As they were quite wide, I used the 8 bore on them, with number 4 shot. I nailed some at nearly 100 yards! It wasn't long before the keepers heard the noise, and came down, and we beat a hasty retreat.

On our way back, we passed one of the keepers' houses, which had a solitary tree beside it. Fred stopped the van, and looked under the tree, and said; 'Look at this, Phil: a lot of pheasants roost in this tree! We'll have some of them tonight.' I said 'What? Right by this keeper's house?' but Fred said he wouldn't hear us. There was so much shit under the tree that Fred thought 40 or 50 pheasants must roost in it.

He had a moderator on his .22, and he said that all I'd have to do was stand under the tree, and, as he dropped them, to put them in a bag. He said we wouldn't start till midnight, and by then the keeper would be asleep.

So back we went, having parked the van about a mile away, and the house was in darkness. He started shooting, and was dropping these pheasants very neatly. They were only about 15 feet up the tree, and the .22 wasn't making much noise, just going 'Plop! Plop!' I said: 'We've got enough, Fred; I've got one bag full up.' He said he'd get a couple more, but then he hit a cock, but didn't kill it, and it came out of the tree crowing and cackling, and of course the lights went on in the house immediately. Again, we beat a hasty retreat back to Selby House.

We had shot quite a mixed bag during our stay, including teal and curlew, which we hung in the bedroom wardrobe. In the morning, the floor was covered in worms that had come out of the curlews' crops during the night.

When we finally got home, unknown to me, Fred had altered the ownership of his car to my name, as I'd said I wanted to buy it, and within days, the police came round, and asked me if I'd been up in the Holbeach area recently. They said they'd had a complaint that the people in the van had been shooting pheasants at night. I denied all knowledge of it, but was so worried that my father would get to hear about it.

I never saw Kenzie Thorpe again. He did a lot with Peter Scott, before Peter stopped shooting and became a conservationist. I can understand that now: I could easily not shoot a duck again now. I never liked shooting tame reared ducks, but I could stop shooting even wild ones now.

CHAPTER 5

EARLY GAMESHOOTING

My father never pushed me into joining the brewery business, but gave me responsibility for the farming operation. Church Farm, adjoining the brewery was 229 acres – mainly dairy, but with pigs, and some arable, too. Very astutely, Father made me a tenant of the farm, so that after his death in 1958, when the brewery was sold to Bass to pay death duties, the new owners were unable to get me out.

Father was always keen on investing in land and property, and when a farmhouse, barn, and 11 acres came up for auction on the edge of the village, he said I should buy it, but I was due to be off on holiday to Spain with some mates when the sale was on. Father thought I should forego my holiday, but I went anyway, and Father bought it in my absence, for £1,400. He told me I should pay him back, which I managed to do, largely by selling some of the land for building. My sister, Barbara, lived in the farmhouse for several years, and eventually the barn was converted into The Sportsman steakhouse.

Earlier, another field had come up for sale which was rented from the local squire, Captain Batten-Pool of Rode Manor. When he died in 1953, tenants had an option to buy their land for £80 an acre, so I bought this 11 acres, and actually paid for it by selling 16 elm trees which were in the hedgerows. My father had a friend in the local Masons, Mr. Holbrow, whom he said would offer me a fair price for the trees. He came to have a look, and then he marked the trees with an 'H', before I had even talked to him about a price. I told my father, who repeated that he'd give the market price for the trees, saying he was a genuine chap.

I was wise enough to get a second offer, from a local timber merchant. He noticed the 'H', and asked if I had already sold them. I replied that no price had been agreed, and that the local should make me an offer. He made an offer, which topped Holbrow's by £500. My father was upset that I had not taken the Mason's offer, but the extra £500 helped clear the total cost of the land.

When my father died, and Fussells was sold, Bass wanted to get rid of the farm, but, with me as sitting tenant, they could only get me out if I didn't pay the rent, or if I was a bad farmer. I made sure I paid the rent, and that the land was farmed well. I offered Bass £30,000 for the farm – far less than the vacant possession value – which they initially turned down, but, three years later, they reluctantly accepted. I was always lucky to have an understanding bank manager, who lent me the money I needed, which was always paid back on time. At that time, the farm supported a herd of 100 cows, which were hand-milked twice a day by six milkers. When Alfa-Laval introduced milking machines, the workforce was cut to two. A pigman looked after 100 sows.

When the brewery was sold, each of the children received 1,000 shares in Bass, and £20,000, making us fairly wealthy by the standards of the time. At the same

PF (front second from right),
with the England Sporting team.

time, Shawford Farm, which adjoined Church Farm, came up for sale, and I bought its 100 acres in 1962, for £14,000. Shawford Farmhouse was let for three years, and I lived with my mother in the village, until I got married.

I was lucky to have a wonderful farm manager called Bert Ingram, who just got on with the work, and allowed me to do even more shooting and fishing.

In the late 1950s and early '60s, our main game quarry was the grey partridge. Farming was different then, of course, with mostly spring drillings, and stubbles left all through the winter. Why are there no English partridges now? Easy: tramlines, and badgers – end of story! Same for peewits, and skylarks. We never saw badgers then; now they're everywhere. Ground nesting birds have little chance, and don't get me started on raptors!

There were few shoots then that reared pheasants, so we relied on greys for our sport; there weren't many redlegs about then. Even farm shoots managed to produce bags of English that today would make headlines. The first 'big' day I went on, we shot 133½ brace, at Lodge Farm, Childrey, near Wantage, which belonged to Colin Matthews, one of our gang. Greendown, belonging to Phil Froude, was next door, and we'd shoot there the next day.

In the Octobers of 1959, '60, '61 and '62 we would shoot four days a week, at such places as Finkley, the Hortons' Widdington at Upavon, Michael Froude's Chain Hill, and Bob Browning's farm at Bishopstone. In 1961, we shot 500 brace one week: I never went home, as we'd socialise hard each evening! The evening after we shot the 133½ brace, I'd shot a lot of partridges, and we drank a lot of whisky. The others found an old rick sheet, and tied me in it, and rolled me down a hill

The Finkley team, 1971. Back row, from left: Mike Lance, Colin Matthews, A. Butcher, PF, Cliff Thorne, Victor Hughes. Front: Bob Strange, Nelson Dance, Bob Browning, 'Buster'.

– and then left me to get out!

If you have a covey of Englishmen coming at you, always shoot at the outside bird first. Most people would take the leader, but then they split, and flare, making the second shot much more difficult. If you shoot the outside bird first, it makes swinging onto the others much easier. The covey was always quite tightly packed; it's different with grouse, where the front bird can be yards ahead of the last. English generally came in coveys, unless they'd been blanked into some roots, when they'd come out singly, rather like redlegs. Then they were easy.

On the old partridge manors, pheasants were vermin. The keepers would go out and kill any pheasant they saw. The hens would drop an egg in a partridge nest, and that was it. The pheasant egg would hatch before the partridge eggs, and the mother partridge would desert the nest with one pheasant chick.

The awful winter of 1962-63 put an end to these wonderful days, and the partridges never really recovered, and people started rearing pheasants instead. Gamekeepers became game farmers, and vermin control became a thing of the past. There's no going back; times have changed, and I've been lucky to see shooting evolve. It's very different today.

Bob Browning remembers: 'My farm at Bishopstone was 1,100 acres. ICI would send someone from the Game Advisory Service (later the Game Conservancy) to count the partridges each spring. The ideal was a pair to every eight acres; our farm had good food for partridges, and we'd generally aim for a pair to every 10 acres. As a comparison, my neighbour was far more intensive, and could only do a pair to 30 acres.

'We generally had a very good line of Guns: we'd all kill right and lefts at greys, though Philip was the star with his Boss – mustard! We used to drink like mad, too. About midnight after one shoot, Philip said he must go, and I went to bed. About 20 minutes later there was a knock on the front door, and Philip was standing there. I thought he must have had an accident, but he'd come back to tell me he'd seen a fox about a mile down the road!'

My first syndicate was at Duxford. John Florey was the farm tenant, near Faringdon. He was a great countryman, and a hell of a character. He used to sit by the fire after shooting, and fall asleep, the steam rising from the ragged plus-fours he wore. He was a big man – he'd been known to carry 7 cwt – and he hardly mounted the gun in his shoulder, he just held it in his big hands. We called him 'Bang, Bang!' as if ever he killed a bird with the first barrel, he'd always give it another! He loved shooting and hunting – he didn't ride, but was always with the terrier men – and followed the Heythrop, the Beaufort, and the Old Berks. He was out all the time.

I'd met John on farm partridge shoots, and in the late 1950s, he started rearing some pheasants under broody hens, and he asked me to join his syndicate. I think it was about £150 a year, and £1 for the beaters – you either took a beater with you, or paid £1.

We shot nearly every Saturday, over three farms – John's Duxford, Richard Wellesley's Buckland, and Major Hornby's Pusey, so we had a fair bit of ground to shoot over. The Hornby family ran W.H.Smith, and Richard was a cousin of the Duke of Wellington; it was much posher company than I was used to, and I had to be on my best behaviour. John Florey did most of the keeping, and his vermin control was rigorous.

Richard had a lovely pair of Purdeys, but his cartridges were awful. They were called Pall Mall, and they were always damp, as you could see the smoke coming out of his barrels when he fired. I used Eley trap shooting 7s at the time, and they were fast cartridges.

One day Richard asked me why it was that he couldn't kill the birds like I could, and I told him I thought he needed to look after his cartridges, as they appeared damp. He couldn't understand this, so I cut open one of them, and poured the powder out in a line, and put a match to it. It spluttered, and eventually burned, but nothing like the quick flash there should have been. He was astonished, and I told him to store his cartridges

Advertising VIRI cartridges in 1985 with skeet champion Brett Newton and world ladies champion Anthea Hillyer

somewhere warm – even on a radiator if he had central heating.

A few weeks later there was an obvious improvement: there was no smoke when he fired, and he was hitting far more birds, and killing them. He was thrilled, and told all his friends about the necessity of warming up their cartridges, and these aristocrats would come up to me and discuss the effects of heating their shells.

I'd learned this a few years before when someone had given me some cartridges to try, and they had been badly stored, as there were specks of rust on the brass caps. Of course, they were all paper-cased then, and you could also tell if they were at all damp, as they quickly swelled up, and were difficult to get into the gun. I had tried these cartridges, and then refused to pay for them, as they were so obviously faulty.

Years later, when I was shooting with Charles Church, he was keen not only on learning to shoot, but the science behind it too. We discussed cartridges, and velocity, and one day, when he came down to see me at home, he noticed boxes of cartridges on the radiators round the house. Intrigued, he asked me why they were there, and I told him of the supposed benefits of warm, dry cartridges. Never one to do things by halves, Churchy organised graphs of the velocities of different cartridges – warm and cold – and compared their performance. There was a noticeable difference in the speed of ignition and muzzle velocity. 'Now I'll be able to shoot like you!' said Churchy.

I remember shooting 13 wigeon at Duxford in the awful January of 1963 with two shots from an old Cogswell and Harrison 8 bore hammer gun. The Thames had flooded, and then frozen, but the duck had kept this area open, and I'd seen the wigeon there when we were shooting. There must have been 20,000 of them: the sky went black as they took off when we started shooting.

The next day, I crawled and crawled along a dyke which led up from the river – with my spaniel attached to my waist with baler twine – and I got to within about 20 yards of the widgeon, before they saw me and took off. I didn't aim at one; I just browned into them. Thirteen fell, but about eight were only wounded, and whenever I sent the dog for them, they dived. Eventually, I had to shoot them again, when they surfaced, with this 8 bore. It took over an hour, and another 10 shots to kill the stragglers! I had some more baler twine, and carried them back, round my neck, so I could show John Florey what I'd done.

That same terrible winter, I went with John and Ken Raines to shoot pigeons which were hammering the sprouts of a market gardener, Tony Slade, near to Duxford. He was in the syndicate as well. The poor birds had virtually nothing to

ON TOP OF THE WORLD

It's a Fiesta for Philip!

How Philip Fussell collected the keys to a £5,500 Ford Fiesta Festival in the 1988 Beretta World Sporting Championship at Apsley, Hants. Mike Barnes reports.

1988 Beretta World Sporting Champion Philip Fussell with his brand new Ford Fiesta Festival.

Right: On his way to victory in an exciting 50 bird shoot-off.

In a marvellous win which saw him collect a brand new £5500 Ford Fiesta, Philip Fussell showed at a stroke how it's possible to mix competitiveness with pleasure and still end up a winner.

And at 57 he also proved that clay shooting really is a sport for all ages. In every way he was a great winner of the 1988 Beretta World Sporting Championship.

The competition more than lived up to the promise of last year's debut. A capacity entry of 750 guns, a tremendous round of 120 sporting targets and three days of glorious sunshine.

To top it all there was again a gripping climax that went to the last gasp. The format saw the top ten guns of both Friday and Saturday plus the top five of Sunday go into a 50 bird shoot-off to decide the medals and the major prizes.

The five stands used were all different from the course itself and a combination of deceptive angles and the

David's shooting stick - Apsley's David Olive checks the line of his targets.

pressure of the prizes at stake, resulted in some very unlikely scores. Targets were dropped almost at will.

The big guns who made the cut-off included Graham Stirzaker (who hit a marvellous 109ex120 on the first day of the competition), A J Smith, Jeremy Welham, George Digweed, Duncan Lawton, Andy Harvison, Mike Reynolds and Martin Elworthy.

But taking an early lead

CHAPTER 6

THE LURE
OF THE WILLOW

I've always loved cricket. I didn't start playing until I went to Monkton Combe as a junior, aged 10, but I took to it straight away, and it wasn't long before I scored my first century against Dean Close, with a Crusader bat that my father had bought me. I started off as a batsman, who also bowled leg-breaks, but as I got taller and stronger in my late teens, I started bowling fast.

I never played any club cricket while I was at school, or when I was working at Bridge Farm. When I went home at weekends, there were always jobs for me to do on the farm. When I returned home to live, I soon started playing for Rode, though, even then, farming sometimes intervened. I remember playing in a needle match against local rivals Westwood, but when I scored 50, I had to go home to help with the milking. It was only five minutes to get home, so I hurried it through, and, when I got back to the ground, we were still batting, and I was allowed to go back in, and completed a century! We won the match as a result.

My father wanted me to play just for the village, but Jack Pearce, the captain of Frome, came and had a chat with me, telling me that I should be playing a better standard of cricket, and he asked me to play for them. They were the best club side in the west of England for years, and I batted number 3 or 4, and also opened the bowling. That was where I met Peter Osborne, who opened the batting, and John Steeds, who was another opening bowler. Both were friends for life.

Another player at Frome, with whom I became great friends, was John Atyeo, who was better known as the Bristol City striker, who – even though they were in the 2nd Division – played six times for England. He scored 351 goals in 645 appearances for City. He was a tremendous athlete, but he asked me to teach him to shoot. I couldn't! He was hopeless. He seemed to have no co-ordination, even though he was a marvellous footballer, and a good club cricketer. Eventually, I told him: 'John, it would take me five years to get you to hit a hayrick in a passage!' We were great mates, and he became godfather to my eldest son, Andrew.

When Harold Gimblett came to play in a benefit match at Frome, there were a good 1,000 people there, as he was quite a star. When Somerset had last played there, he'd batted Number 8, and scored a century in 63 minutes – he'd been told it was his last trial game as he wasn't good enough! He went on to become one of Somerset's greatest batsmen – a wonderful six-hitting opener – and played for England three times.

That was before I became involved with the county, but I was then a 20 year-old, opening the bowling, and, second ball, I clean bowled him with a beautiful cutter. As he walked off past me, he snarled: 'They haven't f*****g come here to watch you, son!'

My successes at Frome got me an invitation to Taunton for a county trial, and I hit 50 against the county attack. The County Secretary, Brigadier Lancaster, asked me if I'd turn professional, and join the county full-time, and I said I'd have to ask my father. He simply said to me: 'Where's that going to get you?' and that was the end of the story: I remained an amateur. In retrospect, he was probably right, but, at the time, I was very disappointed. My father never once watched me play – at school, locally, or for Somerset – although he would sometimes comment on my performances, after reading about them in the local paper.

My first appearance for Somerset was at Weston-super-Mare in August 1953, against Nottinghamshire. It wasn't a great success: I managed to take one wicket in their only innings, as they ran up 252, and then we were out for 94 in our first innings. I batted Number 8, and they had an Australian leg-break bowler called Dooland, who completely did me with his googly, and I was caught at slip for 5.

I'd watched him before I went in, but I couldn't see any change in action. When I got to the wicket, the not-out bat was Johnny Lawrence, Somerset's leg-spinner. He was 20 years older than me, and I said to him: 'I can't see his googly.' Johnny replied: 'Don't worry, son; neither can I!'

We followed on, and I did no better second time round, when I was stumped – again off Dooland – for 5 again. We lost by an innings.

I remember more about the night before the match, when we'd gone out to The Winter Gardens for a dance. I was trying to be sensible, so stuck to orange squash, but Reg Simpson, the Notts (and England) opening bat was there, and he was absolutely legless, and had to be carried out. I thought he'd be easy meat the next morning for us, but he made a very stylish 52. After that I started drinking!

Despite my lack of success, the captain Ben Brocklehurst asked me if I could play in the next three county games. I said I'd have to phone my parents, and check with my father, as it was harvest-time, and I'd be away for the next 10 days. When I phoned, my father said that I was needed back home, as they were having trouble

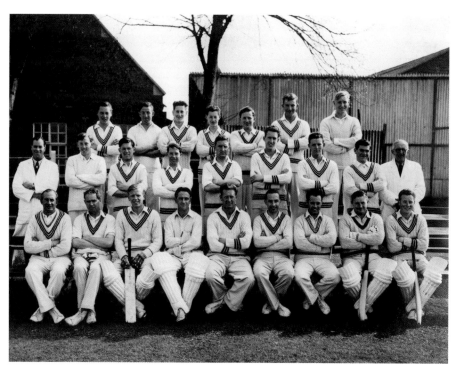

Maurice Tremlett's 1952 Somerset squad,
PF second from the right in the back row

with a new combine – an Allis Chalmers – which kept going wrong. So my first experience of county cricket lasted just one match.

The difference between playing club and county cricket was demonstrated on my return to Somerset in 1956. I'd been playing for Frome, on tour in Sussex, and scored a hundred, when I received a telegram from Somerset, saying they needed me to play in Taunton the following day against Gloucestershire. They booked me a room in the Crown & Sceptre the night before, but I was late getting there, after spending the evening with a young lady, so I ended up over-sleeping in a hayrick!

The next day the ground was absolutely packed, and, when I finally got to the front gate, the gateman wouldn't believe that I was a player as I hadn't shaved. 'You tell Jesus Christ that!' he said, but, luckily, Maurice Tremlett, who was captain, was pacing round the car park at the time, waiting for me, and called to them to let me in. I was the only amateur playing, and so I had a changing room to myself – the professionals and amateurs were segregated then.

When I went out to bat, there was an off-spinner called Sam Cook on. I had a beautiful Gradidge bat, with a wonderful sweet spot, and when he bowled me a half-volley, I absolutely creamed it. Unfortunately, Tom Graveney was standing at silly-mid-off, and stuck a hand down, and caught the ball about an inch off the ground. 'On your way, mate!' he said. I couldn't believe it – out for nought (he may have remembered that when I'd played for Monkton Combe juniors, against Bristol Grammar School, I'd bowled both Tom, and his brother Ken, with my leg breaks).

I opened the bowling with Brian Lobb at the other end, but didn't take any wickets as Arthur Milton scored a century, and then my batting was no better in the second innings, either: another spinner, 'Bomber' Wells, bowled me for another duck, so I bagged a pair. Gloucestershire eventually beat us by one wicket in a tense second innings, but I wasn't called on to bowl.

I played a lot of Second XI and Minor Counties cricket after that, but couldn't commit to playing enough, for the County First XI. They would ring me up and see if I could play, and sometimes I could, sometimes I couldn't. It was easier to play the two day minor county games.

The *Bristol Evening World* commented in 1958: 'If Philip Fussell and John Steeds had been professional cricketers, instead of farmers, they might have opened the bowling for Somerset many years ago.' The article stated that Frome could well have been called the champion side of Somerset for many years, and that 'Philip

Fussell is still there, and what a club cricketer he is. It is a pity that on the rare occasions he has played for Somerset 1st XI, and the many times for the second string, he has not played his natural game and hit the ball. Although Philip is a natural in-swinger and leg-cutter, and consequently always a danger, it is his ability to hit the ball out of the ground which makes him so dangerous in any form of cricket.'

I still played for Frome, until 1967, when my back started being a real problem. My bowling action put a lot of stress on it, and I used to bowl a lot of overs. I used to have a physio at the ground, and he'd give me electro-therapy during the lunch and tea breaks. When I had my first hip done, the surgeon, Roy Preo, said to me: 'I knew you'd be coming to see me!' He was a keen cricketer, and he'd watched me at Taunton, and he knew my action put a lot of strain on my back and hip. He told me my front foot was always splayed, and it always caused problems.

In 1972, I was coaxed out of retirement to play in the Western League at Bath. My farm foreman, Bert Ingram's nephews, David and John, played for Bath, and they kept on at me to play again. Eventually I agreed, on condition that I didn't have to bowl, and could field at first slip. Jane thought I was completely mad.

I hadn't had any practice, but went to a friendly against Devizes, and scored 50. I played the next weekend against Downend in the league, and unfortunately managed to run out Mick Taylor, who later became a good friend, and picked up every week on my shoot at Rydon. He was a teenager then, and I sent him back on what was his call, and he was out by yards. He got back to the pavilion, and asked who the old geezer was, out in the middle. Then, when we were fielding – him at mid-on, and me at mid-off – I twice shouted 'Yours' for 50:50 catches which he then dropped! I said to him: 'You're not having much of a game!' In the bar afterwards, I apologised, and told him: 'I really ought to buy you a pint, young man.' 'You ought to buy me a f*****g barrel!' was his reply.

Another game I remember well from that year was on Bank Holiday Monday, when we played away against Stroud. It had rained heavily overnight, and the pitch was a brute. We were soon in trouble, and I lost my place in the batting order, while looking for a ball that John Ingram had hit into the car park – three wickets fell while I was away! I went in number 8, with the score at 30 for 6. This soon became 44 for 8, and I started to hit out. My back was killing me, and I had to have a runner, which was usually a recipe for disaster, as I had the reputation of being the world's worst caller. When the ninth wicket fell, we had 62, but the number 11 kept

At The Sportsman with John Farrell, through whom I met Jane

whisky like it came out of a tap! He took Lord Hylton's shooting at Ammerdown, near Radstock, and ran that as a private shoot; I'd go there almost every Saturday. He made a lot of money: he had a Ford Eight when he came to Bath, and within three years, he had a Rolls.

He also had a hotel in Montrose. He used to go up there to check on it, and he rang me one day, and said I must come up and do some fishing, and shoot some pigeons. He had the Hatton beat on the North Esk, which had come with the hotel. Even though we were harvesting, I couldn't resist! I got up there by lunchtime the following day, and, when I arrived, I met up with John, who was trying to catch a salmon which had eluded him for some days in one of the pools. He was trying to foul-hook it – totally illegal, but it was his beat – and he was having no luck.

I managed to shoot 131 pigeons on some stubble that afternoon, and when I got back, John was still there. He told me the fish was coming up all the time, but he couldn't get it. After some dinner, he said we must go down again, and that I should try and catch it. I had a good look, and decided the fish must be lying up under a ledge, and then regularly coming up to the surface in the same place. I said to John: 'If you really want that fish, I'll shoot the bugger!' He said: 'What do you mean?' I replied: 'That old cock fish keeps coming up in the same place every five minutes, and if I sit over the far side, I reckon I can have him.'

So I sat there, and the first time he came up, I wasn't quite on him, so I didn't fire. This happened several times, but then he came up absolutely perfectly, and I had him. 7 shot at 20 yards, with a full choke, caused him to splash around a bit, but we netted him as he went downstream, a 22 pounder. He'd obviously been in the pool for some time: he was black, but a fish was a fish to John. He was keen to have another go, as there was another fish in a pool higher up, but I told him that one was enough with a shotgun! There can't be many people who've shot a salmon.

Having seen John Farrell's success, I decided to use some of the money I'd saved, to set up a steakhouse of my own. The farmhouse my father had bought while I was in Spain, had a barn with it, which I decided to convert into the restaurant, which I duly did over the next couple of years, with the help of the men on the farm and a part-time builder. Jane encouraged me to do it: she said she'd run it for me! Sneakily, I copied what Farrell had: Jane knew all the suppliers, so that helped. It took about two years to set up, and I called it The Sportsman.

We opened in January 1965. For the opening night, my butcher friend, Jim Denning, killed a 14 cwt four-year-old steer that had been fattened up on barley and swedes. There was a bit of coverage in the local paper, and a lot of local word-of-mouth. I hoped for 20 to turn up, but 200 did! We ran out of steaks!

We did scampi, lemon sole, T-Bones, rumps and sirloins – with chips and peas; and ice cream. If you wanted coffee, you had to have it at the bar, so the table was freed up. It was a great money-maker: we would do roughly 300 meals on a Saturday night – and during the week, too, in the early days. People parked all the way up the road. In the winter, it was shooters; in the summer, all the local cricket teams, and touring sides, would come in. Turnover was about £2,500 in a good week, and we made £40,000 profit the first year. Hazy days!

My mother was convinced that I was running a knocking-shop! She wouldn't believe me when I said it was a restaurant. She saw me, every evening, counting out the wads of cash, and was sure I was up to no good. On her 80th birthday, though, we finally managed to get her to come for a meal. She liked a dry Martini, or a Babycham, and enjoyed her steak – but she never came again.

Jane was a marvellous hostess, and knew everyone. She loved doing it, and the success was down to her. We had two chefs, and, one Saturday night, both were ill, and Jane sent a message to me while I was playing cricket, saying I had to get back to help out. I did chips, and one grill, and we did 333 meals that night. Some of my friends saw me at work, and asked what was going on. I said I was working for a living!

On 17 May 1965, Jane and I were married, and when Jane became pregnant (with, first, Andrew, and then Timothy, known as 'Titch'), her sister, Tina – who was working in John Farrell's other pub – came and ran it, until she, too, married and went to Rydon, in Devon, with her husband. After that, Jane's mother helped out, and her Aunt Beatrice.

My wedding day, cutting the cake with Jane on May 17, 1965

As other pubs started doing food, competition hit the takings, but The Sportsman kept going until 2000, when it just got too much for Jane, and we leased it out. The next owners went bust, and then we sold the land for housing.

Jane was the best wife I could have had. She loved to work, and she loved me to play, though once, in exasperation, she said to me: 'If I had fish scales on my back, and pigeon feathers in my arse, you'd take more notice of me!' She only came gameshooting with me once. It happened like this: the steakhouse was doing really well, and she'd been working very hard, and I said to her that once the shooting season was over I'd take her on holiday, and she could choose where she wanted to go. She couldn't believe it! She loved the sun, and suggested a cruise. I'd been on a ferry to Ireland once, with Bob Browning, when it had been really rough, and I'd been terribly seasick, so the idea of a cruise didn't really appeal.

But I gave in, and we had a bad time on this cruise, too: a Force 9, off the Azores! Everyone succumbed, except a publican from Scotland, and I asked him for his secret. 'All you've got to do, Philip, is sit at the bar with a bottle of champagne, and, as you drink it, burp all the time!' he told me. It didn't work. I thought we were going to sink.

Anyway, when it calmed down, we met this rich chap from Sussex: Reg Heaver who had a big sand and gravel business, and he had the best cabin on the ship. In the bar, he was half pickled, but he knew my name in the shooting world, and he told me about his shoot in Sussex, where, he claimed, they regularly shot 1,000 good pheasants over two days: this was unheard of at the time. He said I must come and shoot with him.

He took a bit of a fancy to Jane, but she said we'd never hear from him again. He took my address, though, and, sure enough, an invitation soon arrived for the following season, as long as I brought Jane along. It was near Goodwood, and Reg told the other Guns that I was the best Shot in Somerset.

On the first drive, I shot really well. We were only six Guns: four in front, and two behind. We killed about 150 pheasants, and I hardly missed one. The next drive, they blanked a lot of birds into the drive, and, just as it started, a cock pheasant got up from the back, and climbed, and climbed, straight over: it was like a swallow, it was so high. The Guns in front all had a go at it, and then I put the gun up, and killed it stone dead. I told Jane I'd show them how to shoot, and proceeded to miss with the next 50 shots! The wind had got up, and the birds were sliding, and I couldn't read their line. Jane turned to me and said: 'I thought you could shoot!'

It was all round the shooting world in no time, that I'd shot so

A typical 'tongue-out' picture of concentration on the bird, using the Beretta SO3EELL which was made for me

badly on this one drive. The next season, I went again, and, on the same peg, on the same drive, I killed 80 birds. One of the other Guns, who'd witnessed my performance the previous year, came up to me afterwards, and said: 'You've had some practice, young man!'

Soon after we were married, she decided she wanted to come pigeon shooting, and see how I spent all my days. She wanted to shoot, but she'd never fired a gun in her life. I had a 20 bore that I thought wouldn't give her too much of a kick. I set up a hide and the decoys on a wheat stubble, and told her to keep her eyes to the front, and I would tell her when to pull the trigger. I could see a pigeon coming into the decoys, and told her to get ready. I said: 'Wait! Wait! Now fire!' and she fired. She completely missed the one we were both looking at, but at that very moment, another flew by from the right straight into the shot, and it fell stone dead. She never fired another shot, so retired with a 100% success rate.

I took her to Scotland on our honeymoon, to the Bridge of Dun, which just happened to be on the South Esk, a wonderful sea trout river. I had a Jaguar then, and we stopped on the way to the hotel, and I was watching the river. I could see masses of sea trout, and I said I'd have to have a go at them, but I'd be back when it got dark. Of course, at that time of year in Scotland, it doesn't get dark! I was

oblivious to the time passing, but eventually I saw the Jag drive up, and out got Jane, saying: 'Are you ever coming home? Don't you realise it's our honeymoon?' I replied that we had plenty of time for that, but the fish might be gone tomorrow!

She only came fishing with me once, too! It was a lovely summer day, and I suggested that she come down to the River Towy with me. I said I'd rung the ghillie, and the water was right, and she'd see why I enjoyed fishing so much. She said she'd bring her book, and lie in the sun.

The water was perfect, and as soon as I got to the river, I saw a salmon, but I thought I'd leave it, and try downstream first. After an hour with no success, I thought I'd go back and have a go for the one I'd seen. With my first cast, I was into the fish, and I realised I'd left my landing net in the car! I shouted to Jane, but she was laid out in the car with her feet out of the window, not reading her book, as I'd first thought, but fast asleep. I kept playing the fish for about 20 minutes: it was about 16 lb, and it was absolutely knackered, rolling on its side. I was hoarse from shouting to Jane, when I heard this voice: 'Were you calling me, darling?' I said: 'For f**k's sake, bring the landing net.' She came ambling down with the net, and I told her to hold it in the water, and I'd bring the fish to her.

I explained in detail how I wanted her to hold the net, but she was flapping it around like she was catching butterflies. I was hysterical. I shouted 'For f**ck's sake, put the net in the water!' 'Don't talk to me like that!' she said, practically in tears. I told her to come back up, and hold the rod, while I finally landed the fish. 'Don't ever ask me to come fishing with you again' was her final word on the subject.

She had a corgi called Pepper when we were married. One day while I was playing cricket, Pepper got into the rearing pen, where I had several broodies, and about 200 pheasant chicks. Pepper killed all the chicks and one of the hens. Jane was distraught, but I said I'd just get some more pheasants. I decided to get my own back on Pepper, though. We had a lot of corn under a shed up at Church Farm, and we surrounded it with bales, and there were soon plenty of rats there. I took Pepper up there, and started lifting the bales. Pepper was deadly, and killed them like lightning. As soon as she'd killed one, she'd be on to the next.

River Towy – Jane's only salmon fishing adventure
(Photograph: Matt Harris)

CHAPTER 8

SHAWFORD SHOOT

In 1978, I was interviewed by *Shooting* magazine, touching on different aspects of the sport, including syndicates. Belonging to a syndicate costs money, and people obviously expect value for money. But it's not always easy to define 'value'. To some it means the number of birds on the gamecart at the end of the day, but to others it means good sporting birds, well shown – and well shot!

This doesn't mean that I'm against syndicates, for without the injection of cash a great many shoots would have disappeared. However, there is always a danger that pressure from people lacking a country background will undermine both the quality and the ethics of the sport as understood by the true countryman.

I was also asked about the sort of shoot I most enjoyed. I said that I tended to favour those organised by owner-occupiers who put on a shoot, not only as a social occasion, but also as an opportunity to try and show better birds for their friends. Presentation is far more important than the size of the bag, and the Guns understand and appreciate the effort.

When I bought Shawford, it made a combined holding, with Church Farm, of 330 acres. I managed to add odd bits to it over the years, like 21 acres adjoining

Shawford, originally owned by the Millett brothers, John and Geoff. They were no farmers really, and, after milking one day, I met Geoff in the pub. I asked him what he was going to do with the ground, as he never seemed to do anything with it, and I said: 'I'll buy it off you. I'll give you a good price for it.' I then offered to spoof him for it: if he won I'd give him £160 an acre; if I won, £80 an acre.

So we spoofed, and I won, so I got the 21 acres for £1,680. I got my solicitor to sort out the paperwork, and I gave him a cheque, thinking that if I paid him, it would be difficult to renege on the deal. The problem was, he owned the land jointly with his brother, with whom he didn't really get on. He should have agreed it with him.

A couple of weeks later, brother John turned up at the house, in tears. He said his brother had no right to sell the land, and he wanted it back. I told him that as far as I was concerned, I had bought the land perfectly legally, and his solicitor backed this up.

The 21 acres was in three fields, and I wanted the internal hedges taken out, so that it was one 23-acre field. I knew another chap who had an earth-removing business, and I asked him if he'd rip out the hedges, and, what he'd charge me. He said it would be £100 – so I offered to spoof him for that, double or nothing. I won that spoof, too!

That field – now still called Millett's – has been a big money-spinner, as the new bypass went straight through it. I had a pheasant pen in the bottom of the field, and managed to get compensation for the damage to the shoot – of £25,000! Then, when the road went through, I got £80,000 for the whole farm, which went a long way to paying off my overdraft.

I decided to set up a driven shoot here, so I could entertain my very generous friends. We'd always had a rough shoot on Church Farm, but I now decided to put a few pheasants down. I did all the keepering myself, and put down about 400 birds, to provide enough for a social shoot. We'd do a duck drive off the lakes at Church Farm, and probably kill 70 or 80 mallard and teal, and then do some pheasant drives.

We killed 130 off one drive once, with one beater – me! It was out of one piece of maize, and the drive lasted about 90 minutes. They were quite good pheasants too, as the pen was about 500 yards down the hill behind the Guns. I had one of my men standing on the hedge which ran alongside the maize, and I'd quietly tap the pheasants into the hedge. When he'd seen about 10 birds go in there, he'd raise his hand, and I'd go forward, and tap them out of the hedge. Then we'd repeat the process. The Guns kept thinking the drive was over, but I'd shout at them that there were more to come. Then we had a drink!

I'd only put 300 birds in that pen, so it was quite a success. We'd always kill more than 50% of what I'd put down, though there were some wild birds, too. I didn't allow any hens to be shot in January, and always got some young broods. I'd always pull back when I was combining, if I saw a young brood in the corn. Now there's so much time pressure on farming activities that they just have to get on with it.

I'd run some tunnel traps, and catch stoats and, mostly, rats. I'd wait all day if I thought there was a crow working the area. Of course, there weren't buzzards then, either. There weren't the numbers of badgers then, or red kites. What chance has a ground-nesting bird got nowadays?

One of the worst predators here is the mink. I've killed 60 over the last 20 years on one part of the river here. I use Fenn traps, and cage traps. If you've got them in the area, you'll catch them within a week. I've caught two silver ones, too. I allow the minkhounds through as well, and they always catch one.

George [Digweed] was here one day, soon after I got to know him. I was showing him one of the pheasant pens, when we saw something coming up the outside of the pen: it was a mink. I told George to watch it, while I went back and got my guns – I had a .22 and a 12 bore with me. Just as I got back, George told me the mink had gone down a rat hole, but then it started swimming across the river. I had the .22 in my hand, and started shooting at it, but it turned back to the bank, and down another hole. I covered the hole with a spade, and told George to get the 12 bore, which I'd left by the pen. When he came back, I started digging, and bolted the mink – which didn't get past George!

I get bad losses now from the road which runs through the farm. Then, there just wasn't the traffic, but now, where I have a strip of maize alongside the road, it's nothing to go out in the morning, and see half a dozen birds squashed.

I did try partridges once, about 10 years ago. Robin Pardoe had some spare, and gave me 200 redlegs. I wasted more time on those birds than I care to remember. I asked Andy Puttock for advice and got some sections to make a pen, but when I released them, I had sparrowhawk problems. Then I had fox problems: up one hedge near where I'd released the partridges, I snared six in a week. We never even saw many partridges, let alone shoot many, on shoot days! Robin kept asking me about how I was getting on with the partridges. I told him: 'Don't talk to me about f**king partridges!'

I reared a white cock pheasant once. It was really quite tame, and you could drive right up to it. In January, we were shooting cocks only, and I told the Guns not to shoot the white one. The sun was behind the drive, so it was quite difficult to see what was what, but I told the Guns that cocks should be shot at whatever height – even if they were walking! I was back gun, behind a local, Frank Shellard, who missed a couple, which I shot, and then he let a couple of quite low ones go by, without firing. I yelled out to Frank to shoot them, and then he ignored the next one that came out, too. I was angry by now, so I shot it without thinking, and it fell at my feet, a white ball of feathers. What a cheer went up from all the others!

My eldest son, Andrew, enjoyed shooting from an early age, though I almost put him off for good, the first time I took him out. He was only about 18 months old, and I told Jane that I could see he wanted to come shooting, and I took him off to a wood on the farm, where, for the next hour and a half, he howled. I took him home, and told Jane I couldn't stand his crying, and she took off his little red wellies, and his feet were blue: he was freezing cold!

Another of me shooting my
beautiful Boss

Despite this, I bought him a .177 air rifle when he was about six, and we had a little rifle range in the house. I took him out pigeon shooting then, and he'd sit in the hide, and shoot any of the walking wounded with the air rifle. It kept him occupied, and he really felt involved. I then got him a .410, rather like the one I'd used as a child. I'd take him to Bill Joyce's local skeet shoot, and he did well off the low tower. After that, he used a lovely little single barrel side-lever Lang .410, which he's used to teach his kids to shoot, too.

He then came shooting with me every day he could. I taught him what I knew. He reminds me often how I used to say 'Let 'em come in!', so he could shoot at a sensible range with his .410. He had to learn to make the first shot count, and kill with confidence. We then used to try and shoot together when several birds came in at once. It's never easy: you agree 'I'll take the one on the right; you take the left,' and then they'd cross over in their final approach!

One day I went looking for more pigeons, and I left my Browning, and told Andrew he could use it while I was gone. He was only about eight at the time.

He told me he could hardly lift it, and he'd rested it on a barbed-wire fence. A pigeon came in, and he pulled the trigger... and ended up on his back on the ground. The pigeon flew off unscathed!

He shot his first 100 pigeons at Pimperne. He told me over the radio that he thought he'd got 100, but we only picked up 98, so we had to wait there while he killed another two. He was using the Bettinsoli 12 bore I won at the Bath & West. It had improved cylinder and full choke, and Andrew complained that the open choke barrel was useless for pigeons. I took the

I shot the white one – how embarrassing
(Photograph: Charles Sainsbury-Plaice)

gun, and one flew past, well over 40 yards up, and I killed it so that it never moved, but just crashed down. I handed him the gun back without a word. He's turned into an excellent all-round shot over the years.

We've had some wonderful days here over the years, and Jane always put on a fantastic spread for our guests. The social side has always been as important for me, if not more so, than the shooting.

Ken Raines remembered a day at Shawford with Philip: 'We shot ducks in the morning, and then went on and shot partridges in the afternoon. We were by a bit of kale, and there was a litter of fox cubs in it – almost fully grown – and Fussell was shouting 'Look out: they're coming!', and he shot one that rolled over and died in front of me. I was a keen hunting man, so didn't really want to shoot a fox.

'I was down there with John Florey, whom I'd picked up that morning in my old Oxford, and, on our way home, I said to him: 'I can't half smell fox!' and, when we got to his home, and we opened the boot to get his ducks out, there was Charlie, laid out on top of them!'

CHAPTER 9

CLAY PIGEONS

A s mentioned, my co-author, Rupert, interviewed me in 1978 for an article in *Shooting* magazine: 'Although I enjoy clay shooting and shoot to win, I sometimes find that competitors take things far too seriously for my taste, and for this reason I much prefer the relaxed friendly atmosphere of game shooting.'

Even when I started clay shooting, it was very competitive, but nothing like it is now. Now it's professional. I didn't shoot clays that much early on, because I was playing cricket in the summer, which was my first love, and there wasn't much clay shooting in the winter months.

Then I started doing a few clay competitions, mostly local – and I won most of them. Even if the prize was only £5, it bought a few cartridges. Then I joined the CPSA, and I shot quite a lot of 'Sporting'. I did some Down-the-Line but found it too repetitive and mechanical. I could shoot 100 straight with my eyes closed! I think that was one of the problems with clays: I just didn't find them that challenging. I preferred real pigeons, or game, and the socialising that went with it.

There was an incident at Finkley in the early days, which rather summed up clay pigeon shooting for me. Nelson put on a DTL competition every year, which was well attended, and became part of the selection for the national squad. I just went along because Nelson wanted me to be there, and to help raise money for the local charities that benefited. I smoked a pipe at the time, and, after I'd shot, I was tapping my pipe out on the metal frame the shooters stood in. My neighbour was offended by this, and told me in no uncertain terms that he was trying to concentrate, and get in to the national team, and would I mind not trying to distract him with my pipe! The next year, I told Nelson I'd give him a donation, but to forget the DTL.

At the West London Shooting Ground there was a competition called the Walker Parker Cup for anyone who had never won a major competition. I went up with Fred Cooper, who said that we should enter. I'd never been up to London before. He told me he'd drive, and that we should start at three o'clock in the morning. We got to Uxbridge, and got lost, but finally got there, and, after telling them I'd never won any competitions, I entered, and won the Cup!

I met Percy Stanbury there, and he asked me how much clay shooting I did. I replied not much, but that I did a lot of pigeon shooting. The following year, I told Fred that we ought to go up again, and he reminded me that I couldn't go in for the Walker Parker, as I'd won it the year before. I said; 'Well, what about the main shoot?'

So I entered the British Open, and ended up Runner-Up! The winner was the very experienced Joe Wheater – after a shoot-off on the High Tower. I shot them as a driven bird, but Joe shot them as crossers – as a lot of pheasant Shots do, nowadays – which I

Another world title, this time as a veteran

71

don't agree with. I got 19 out of 20, but Joe killed all 20, but behind him, when they'd finished flying. Old man Browning, who had seen a lot, said 'Joe, why didn't you shoot 'em like the boy shot them? They're supposed to be driven pheasants!'

One year, I won a competition called the Richmond Watson Cup – or I thought I'd won it. I'd filled the cup with Guinness at lunchtime, and had celebrated hard, before they announced that there would be a shoot-off, on the rabbit stand. By now, I was completely incapable of hitting these rabbits, and eventually they were rolling them out by hand, slowly, and I still couldn't hit them. It was just good fun then. Now, it's such big business, everyone takes it much more seriously.

Terry Clarke and 'Ginger' Chatfield were two of the local lovable rogues – both good Shots, and great fun, but dangerous. They used to take me clay pigeon shooting on a Sunday. One day, I came home and said to Jane: 'I'm never going with those two again. If they come round, you must tell them I'm out!' I'd won the competition, but we went in Ginger's convertible Mercedes, and I was in the back. They were chatting away, but I could hear this strange knocking noise coming from the back. I told them, but they took no notice, and told me to go back to sleep.

A few seconds later, the back wheel came off, the car lurched to one side, and the wheel overtook us going down the road! 'No problem!' they said, and flagged down the next car that came along, whose inhabitants helped lift the Merc so that the spare wheel could be put on, as they didn't have a jack. I'd had enough, so the next week I hid my car, and went upstairs when I heard them arrive. Jane told them I was out, but they didn't believe her, and Clarky said: 'He's in the house somewhere!' and they started to search for me. I got under the bed! The next thing I heard Clarky say: 'If you're hiding under the bed, your feet shouldn't stick out!' They pulled me out, found my gun, and bundled me into the car, and off we went again.

Clarky invited me for a day at Shoscombe, where there weren't many birds, but a lot of socialising. The main drive of the day was lunch, accompanied by quite a few gin and tonics – my favourite tipple! I could see they were trying to get me drunk, so I surreptitiously started emptying half of each of my drinks on the floor. Even so, we staggered out of the pub for the afternoon drive, and they told me to go Back Gun behind everyone else. There were some quite good Shots there, and not much got through, until the final bird of the drive got up: a hen, right from the back of the cover on the hill above us. She soared into the sky, over the wires between two pylons, and I think every Gun in front had two shots at her, and missed. She came straight over me, though, and I nailed her: it must have been one lucky pellet, as she

we stopped at a betting shop, and each had £5 each way on it. Five minutes later, I said I thought we should put a bit more on, and we placed another tenner each. We stayed in the bookies for the race, and the horse came in second, at 20-1. We paid for our entire holiday with those bets.

Our next foray was to the Towy, and I started fishing the Junction Pool, where the Cothi meets the Towy. It was a very good pool, and I finally caught a salmon, which I took down to show Bob, who was fishing The Flats, which was a good pool for sea trout. We swapped over; Bob told me later he'd gone up to the Junction Pool, knowing that I'd probably flogged it to death in my eagerness. To get to the pool, you had to get over a stile, and then a ditch about four feet wide, which had about a foot of water in it.

He had a tin of worms, and added a worm to his fly, and almost immediately had a fish on. He brought the fish down to show me, and I asked him where he'd got it. He replied that it had been in the ditch, just where it joined the river. I didn't know any better, and believed him!

The next day, Bob asked me where I wanted to fish, and I said I'd go back up to the Junction Pool. I didn't realise he was watching me, as I fished the ditch for about an hour – with no success. I told Bob that he was pretty lucky to have got a fish out of the ditch, as there was so little water in it. Bob said that was what fishing was all about: sometimes you got lucky. He didn't tell me the truth until about five years later.

One of the funniest stories was when we were fishing the Dovey. The river was low, and I knew that if we could find a deep pool, there would be fish there. We found just such a pool, right at the top, and I could see it was stuffed with sea trout, and salmon. I could see their tails waving in the water – their heads were under an overhang. I could stretch down and touch them, and they didn't spook. There were so many fish there, that they just thought it was another one touching them. Bob was on the far bank, and I told him to cast his fly over; I took it and felt along the first fish, and as he opened his mouth, I slipped the hook in to his 'scissors', and shouted: 'You're in, Bob!'

He played the first fish, and got it out: a 14lb sea trout. I then did it again…and again. The first four were all sea trout – all double-figure fish. I said: 'Let's have a good one before we go!' I could feel the last fish I went for was either a very big sea trout, or a salmon, and again I hooked it, before Bob played it, and I netted it. It was a 21lb salmon. Then we scarpered with the fish in the boot of the car, hoping the bailiff didn't catch us.

(Photograph: Marcus Janssen)

Another time, we were after sea trout, but the water was low, and there wasn't much chance of a fish. It was pretty dark, and there were some Germans fishing in a pool below where we were. I was using a single-handed rod, and I caught my fly in an ivy-covered tree on the far bank. Bob came up, and I told him that I was in, and started playing the 'fish'. Soon the Germans came up to watch: I said it must be a big fish on, as he was boring down the river. After about 10 minutes, I broke, and the 'fish' got away, amid much sympathy from the Germans, and from Bob, who never caught on till I told him some time later.

We'd go with our families, and young children, on holiday down to Wales. The girls and kids would go to the beach, and we'd go fishing. I remember one week, the bathroom was out of commission the whole time, as the bath was full of sea trout.

Another great fishing friend is Peter Stratton. He got me into a timeshare on the Conon, which was great fun for many years, and now he's a member of the Spey syndicate I still fish with every summer. We've had a lot of laughs together: he's a great naturalist, a natural Shot, and an excellent fisherman. My old friend and near-neighbour, John Long, had come up with us for a week on the Beauly. Longy was a dry old stick, and rarely cracked a smile, let alone a laugh. The river was low, and salmon were scarce, and Longy didn't have much luck. On the Wednesday, he'd retired to the hut for lunch, and I was walking back, having finally caught a 2lb trout and a salmon of about 8lb, when I met up with Peter, who asked me how I'd got on. I showed him my two fish, and told him that I was going to have a laugh with Longy. I hid the fish beside the hut, and went inside to see Longy's long face. 'Any good?' he asked me. 'Yes' I said, 'I've had two.' 'Two what?' said Longy, 'Trout, I expect. I bet you haven't caught a salmon?' 'How much do you want to bet?' I asked him, and he replied, '£100'. I told him I needed a proper bet, and he raised it to £500. 'How about £5,000?' I said, and he finally agreed.

I went outside and picked up my fish, and stood by the window, and slowly held up the trout. Longy said 'I knew it was only a trout, Fussell – get your chequebook out!' I smiled and lifted my other hand, with the salmon in it. 'How about 'ee then, Longy!' I said. 'Get your chequebook out!' I never did get paid, but it was worth it, just to see his face.

On another occasion, we decided to wind up Lloyd Stone, another member of my Spey syndicate. We were then fishing the Conon, and Peter and I put together this story of a 70-year-old woman fishing a pool called the Ferry Stream, as we knew Lloyd was going there the next day. We told him that she was in her slippers, but that she must have known what she was doing, as she was Spey-casting, with an old greenheart rod, a good 40 yards across the river into the pool on the far side – and that she'd caught three fish while we'd been watching.

The next morning, Lloyd skipped breakfast, and when we went down to the river, there he was – an excellent caster – trying to reach the pool from the near side, and not getting anywhere close!

Peter Stratton remembered:

'Phil and I were fishing the Conon in June one year. I had had a blank morning, and walked down to where Phil was fishing a pool called The Major. He had waded

The Spey syndicate – standing, from left: Lloyd Stone, Bob Kane, Paul Weiss.
Seated, from left: Freddie Clayton, PF, Stephen Brandt (head ghillie), Peter Stratton

in quite deep, and was concentrating with his usual ferocity – mouth open, tongue out, eyes on his fly – and hadn't noticed my arrival. There was a gorse bush on the bank directly behind him, and I lay down flat behind it, and gave a loud squeak, shaking the bush as I did so. He briefly turned round, but – seeing nothing – returned to his fly. I repeated the performance, giving my best otter impersonation, and he looked harder this time.

'I did it once more – louder this time – and gave the gorse a really good shake, and finally caught his attention. He wound in his line, and very slowly approached the bush, head forward, eyes fixed. I squeaked again, and, as he peered down – his head practically touching the gorse – I leapt up. In his surprise he launched himself backwards, and fell into the river, before calling me all sorts of unmentionable things, and then exploding into the Fussell cackle.'

I've fished the Moy in Ireland for years now, as Norman Marshall's guest, and I've been in my syndicate on the Spey for 20 years: we fish the Ballindalloch beat, and it's one of the best. The thing with salmon fishing is that the water's got to be right, and, when it is, you've got to go! The ghillie on the Thurso would ring me up, and say that the water was rising. I'd drop everything, and go – it was a 700 mile drive to get there, but it's a fantastic river. I'd be up there catching fish, and I'd send them, by rail, back home, and Jane would be serving them in The Sportsman the next day. It would be marked up as 'Caught by the Landlord'. The customers loved it!

If I had one day of sporting left in my life, I'd choose to spend it fishing the Beat 2 on the Thurso in the first week in August – as long as the water was right! I met Lord Thurso, and we got on really well. He said to me: 'Philip, you can fish Beat 10 (his private beat) any time you want to!' Marvellous!

What I've always loved about fishing is that you need just as much fieldcraft to catch a wily salmon, as you do to make a bag of pigeons. I remember one occasion on the North Esk, where there were overhanging water elders all down the stretch under the Hatton Pool, and the fish were lying there. They'd been fished hard in the pool itself, and I asked the ghillie how deep the water was there, and he replied 'Too deep, Sir.' It was after a spate, and the fish did not want to be caught in the usual pools, so I told the ghillie I was going to have a go at getting at these fish.

I managed to do a little flick cast under the elders, and, during that week, I had 21 salmon from that stretch! The ghillie couldn't believe it, but I said to him that the fish simply hadn't seen a fly down there before; in the faster water, they were

The South Esk – honeymoon river!
(Photograph: Andrew Graham-Stewart)

always seeing flies, but never under those elders. Bob Browning was there, and he didn't catch a fish all week.

In those days, of course, I was steady on my legs, and I could get myself out of trouble; now I sometimes think – halfway across a river – 'You bloody idiot, Fussell. What are you doing here?' I nearly drowned on the Moy a few years ago. I'm a bit unsteady now that I've had new hips! I had my wading stick, but the water had washed a hole out that I stepped into, and I lost my balance completely. I tugged at my life jacket toggle, but it didn't inflate. As I lost my footing, I managed to grab the branch from an overhanging withy tree. I dropped the brand new Hardy rod I was using, and just hung on to the tree. Luckily, the ghillie wasn't far down the river below me, and saw my rod floating past, and realised what had happened. He came up in the boat, and managed to get me to the bank.

Howard Bennett reminisced about his first fishing expedition – Beat 2 on the Thurso – with Philip:

'When I first started taking an interest in salmon fishing, in the early '90s, Philip invited me up to fish on the Thurso. He was well in with the head keeper, who would ring him up whenever the river conditions looked good, and the fish were running. Philip would just drop everything, and go – often driving through the night, to get to Caithness, which was a good 10 hour drive, with only short stops.

'We got to the hotel, late in the evening, and had a quick dinner. I had driven all the way, and was tired out. I said to Philip: 'I'll see you at breakfast.'

'No time for breakfast! We'll be off early!' he replied.

'What time is early?

'Four o'clock,' he replied. 'Come to my room, and I'll have made a cup of tea, and we'll go on!'

I wasn't over-thrilled by the thought of this, as I got into bed just before midnight, and even less thrilled when I realised soon after that the town hall clock was right opposite my window, and it chimed on the hour. Having heard it chime 12, one, two and three, I hardly slept a wink, and was up at 3.30, and knocking on Philip's door promptly at four. True to his word, the tea was waiting, and, after a quick cuppa, we were off.

'We're going to Beat 2, Howard,' he said.

'Is that any good?'

'Yes, it's the best, and we should have some luck today.'

After a drive of about 15 minutes, we parked up in a gateway. Dawn was just visible, but it was still pretty dark. I thought we should wait till we could see a bit more, but Philip was adamant that he knew where the river was: 'I know these old moors like the back of my hand. You just follow me,' and he strode off.

I quickly grabbed my gear, and followed his now distant figure in the gloom. 'Hang on, Phil,' I shouted, but he just told me to keep going, and then he disappeared! I stopped and looked, and all I could see was the tip of his rod, gently waving out of the deep ditch he'd fallen into.

'Bloody hell, How,' he shouted, 'I didn't know that was there.'

'And you know these moors like the back of your hand!' I reminded him.

Finally we started fishing, and we carried on, without much success, till 9.30, when Philip suggested we went back to the hotel for breakfast. Everything had been cleared away by then, but, turning on the Fussell charm, Philip persuaded them to give us some breakfast. Philip had two of everything: cornflakes, toast, and everything fried you could imagine – with extra fried bread.

Afterwards, he told me that there were the makings for a picnic laid out, and that I should put together enough for our lunch, and some beers, and then we returned to the river. He then fished, right through, until early evening. When he's fishing, he's totally focussed on catching the next fish. He just casts, for hours on end – not a pretty cast, but clinical – and he covers every inch of his water.

I was a real novice, but, late in the morning, I get a fish on – not a big one: about a 6lb grilse – Philip was about 100 yards up the river from me, and I called to him to help me land this fish. Either he was too deaf to hear me, or he was too focussed on what he was doing. I was on the bank which was several feet above the water level. I managed to find a spot where I could slide down the bank onto some gravel, still hoping that Philip would come to help, but then he caught a fish, too.

I knew then that I was on my own. He has a regular habit, that when he catches a fish, of netting it, despatching it (which you could do then; he still doesn't really approve of Catch and Release!), removing the fly, and then he has a way of stroking a fish, smoothing it out, admiring his good work, and evaluating the fish.

He went through this whole process with his fish, and I thought that surely now he would come and help me, but, no, he put another fly on, and started fishing again, completely oblivious! I eventually managed to haul the fish across to where I was standing – by now the poor fish was completely knackered – and I eventually landed it by myself. Looking back, I think he ignored me so that I would learn the fastest way: by doing it myself. I did get him back some years later, when he was in a difficult position, and I sat and watched as he struggled. When he said later: 'You could have helped me!', I reminded him of this occasion on the Thurso.

We fished through the afternoon, and I was getting pretty tired, eventually suggesting that we should stop for our picnic, but, by then, Philip decided that we should return to the hotel for dinner, which sounded a good idea to me. The restaurant was empty, but, again, Philip persuaded them to rustle up whatever dinner they could provide us with. We had a couple of drinks, and I relaxed, thinking 'What a day!', and getting a nice rosy glow at the thought of my bed.

'Right! We're off!' said Philip.

'We're off?' I queried.

He said: 'We'll get another one tonight if we're lucky.' And he made me drive back, yet again, to the river. The light was going, but my heart wasn't in it – I was truly knackered. But I was five years younger than him, and wouldn't give in, so I soldiered on, but it was a physical task. We didn't catch anything after dinner, either: it hadn't been a very productive day. He'd caught two, and I caught one.

It was after midnight when he decided to call it a day, and then we couldn't find the car in the dark! We finally made it back to the hotel at about one o'clock.

'It's alright, How,' he said, 'Not so early tomorrow. Half past three should do!'

I was ready to explode, as he followed up 'Yes, we're on a different beat tomorrow, and it's a longer drive, so we'll need to get off earlier!' It was only when he started chuckling that I realised, thankfully, that he was pulling my leg, and he said 'Don't worry, I'll see you at breakfast.'

I was so tired that not even the town clock disturbed my slumbers that night. I was unconscious. That was my first day of salmon fishing – about 22 hours of it!'

CHAPTER 11

IT'S NOT JUST ABOUT PULLING THE TRIGGER

I've made a lot of friends over the years, and I'm still shooting with some, 40 or 50 years on. I've already mentioned several, and there are others who have played a large part in my life.

I've shot on Robin Pardoe's Tetton shoot for nearly 40 years. It's in the Quantock Hills, just north of Taunton. You get some wonderful pheasants there. I'm now the oldest member of the syndicate, and many of my old friends who shot there have died. Robin's a great character, and was one of the original 'A-Team' when Charles Church set it up. He no longer shoots, and I've said to him that I really can't go on shooting there, but he won't hear of me dropping out.

I first met him at Sydling, in Dorset, which was then run by Reg Smith. I'd never shot there before, and was introduced to Robin, who was very smartly turned out – public school, you know – but he hadn't done much driven shooting. The first drive we did, I was back gun, right behind him, as he'd drawn number five. Well, he shot, and shot, and shot, and might have killed two or three, but I had a hell of a drive: Wallop! Wallop! Wallop! They just rained down.

The classic thing was when the roles were reversed about 15 years later: we were shooting Molland Wood, and Robin was placed behind me, and I was really on song. They were raining down all round him! At the end of the drive, he came up to me and said: 'You bastard!' I asked what the problem was, as I must have left a lot of birds for him. He said: 'There were five pheasants coming out together, and you went Whack! Whack! Reloaded, and had the next two, and even got the last bugger, which hit me in the back!' I killed nearly 100 pheasants on that drive, and I think Robin got two.

I still really enjoy Tetton. Only last season I had a truly memorable time: we were doing Dowager's, a lovely drive, where the birds curl over a plantation on the top of a bank, and head back to The Knoll where the pen is. I was on a great peg for the wind that day, and where the birds are highest. I had young Toby Bennett with me, and he helped by stuffing my cartridges. I told him to count how many I shot, as I thought I was in for a good stand. He asked me how I knew where they'd come, and I told him that I'd shot there for nearly 40 years, so I should know how they'd fly.

At the end of the drive, I asked him what I'd killed, and he replied: 'You killed 39... with 45 shots.' They were just on the right line, so I could stay on my seat, and not have to try and shoot on my left, which is very difficult for me. We killed 186 birds on that drive, not bad for the shoot in January, and not bad for me aged nearly 84!

Howard Bennett became a great friend. He had an abattoir in the '60s, and I'd just started the steak house, so he supplied a lot of our meat. He had only recently started shooting, and I drew next to him at Finkley. He'd had an operation to replace his hair, and had a hat on. He couldn't hit the lowest pheasants, and he asked me for help. I told him what to do: he did it, and he started hitting them – and we became great mates. He learned to fish, too, so we've shared a lot of happy times.

Sadly, a lot of my old friends are dead. I shot pigeons and game with my neighbour, John Long, for years. He came to dinner on my 83rd birthday, went home, and died in his sleep. John Long's father used to drive round in his Land Rover, with an old 12 bore hammer gun, cocked! We were sitting in the back, and eventually had to ask Longy to tell his father at least the hammers should be down, at the very least. He was scared of his father, so wasn't happy about telling him, but we insisted, as we'd ride more comfortably. His father was most offended, saying that the gun wouldn't go off with the hammers at half cock.

I was shooting with them once, and we got down to their best drive, which was

The Best Game Shots in the Land – in 1993 *The Field* nominated their 1stX1 with this painting by John Paley.
From left: Hugh van Cutsem, Duke of Roxburghe, David Olive, Caspar MacDonald-Hall, Tony Ball, PF, Ned Goschen, Phil Burtt, Jim Albone, Basil Kinch, Duke of Northumberland (then Lord Ralph Percy)

a strip of kale on a hill, from where the birds were driven back to a wood behind the gunline. The only problem was: the wood belonged to the neighbouring estate, Major Duckworth's Orchardleigh, and the pheasants had been enticed into the Longs' kale. There was no love lost between the Longs and their neighbour, and old man Long would place Peter Osborne and me in the prime spots between the flushing point and the wood. 'I don't care if they're running along the ground,' he'd say, 'Shoot 'em!'

The neighbouring keeper, Fred Hunt, would stand in the wood, tearing his hair out. 'Young Fussell,' he'd call out, 'Let some go! They're not Mr. Long's pheasants; they're mine!' I never actually shot one on the ground, but not many got through. Old man Long would always notice if any escaped, and tell you all about it.

I met John Steeds playing cricket at Frome. He had Dropping Lane Farm near Bruton, and then became a tenant of Lord Oxford's at Mells, where he took over Branch Farm from Peter Osborne's father. He ran a nice little shoot on the farm; he keepered it himself, as we all did. It was a typical shoot of the time: if we shot 100 pheasants it was a red-letter day, and we'd then play cards into the night. I introduced him to his wife, Jean, and I was best man at their wedding.

I've shot with Basil Kinch for years, too; latterly, I've shot at Halse, near Taunton, for over 20 years, but originally he had a farm up in the Cotswolds. I remember leaving there with John Steeds, late one evening, after much socialising: John had a Morris Isis car, and soon after we left, the fog came down. You could hardly see 10 yards. We kept seeing signs saying 'Castle Combe 1½ miles', and John said: 'I'll be okay if we get there, as I know my way home!' but we never found it. We went round and round in circles – we went through Colerne several times – and finally got home about 5am, after the fog lifted.

I've shot a lot with Ray Hillyer – both game and clays. We were shooting at Bickleigh, near Plymouth in 1986, where Ray ran the shooting for Brian Mears. A keepering friend, Bob Smallman, was there, and on the second drive I was number 7, and Bob was 8. Normally that was a back gun, but the wind was blowing hard, and, unknown to me, Ray placed Bob about 80 yards beyond me, though out of sight. The birds flew really well along the valley, and Ray told me no-one had ever really done them justice.

Maurice Pearce had come down as he was going to help run some of the shoots, and he stood with me to watch the drive in progress. I told him to have a couple of cartridges handy, in case there was a flush. I shot like a dream, and killed 10 birds on the trot.

Ray told me later that he began to hope there would be a flush, so that Bob would have the chance of one bird, at least. Towards the end of the drive, two birds came out together, and there was another 50 yards behind, but I killed the first two perfectly, and said 'One, Maurice!' who quickly loaded one shell, and I killed the third bird, too. We were having a drink at the end of the drive, and when Bob trudged back, I asked him how he'd got on: 'Well, I didn't need a f*****g loader, Phil!' he replied.

Laurence Gardner's been a great friend, too. He's been very successful in business, and he takes a couple of days at Glenstriven each year, from Peter Blacker. I remember shooting at Bleasdale, and Laurence was next to me in the line, and very nervous. I'd never met him before, but he was a friend of Norman Marshall.

Bill Joyce and Norman were back Guns. The first eight birds came over, and we shot them all. The drive went on, and we carried on killing them. Bill and Norman hardly had a shot.

That night Laurence and I stayed up till one o'clock, and reminisced over a whole bottle of brandy. He was not well the next day, but I was okay: I've always had a strong head.

I've shot at Prescombe many times now, through the kindness of Steve Thomas. It's a great shoot, and he's a great host, and he's been very generous to me. He always has a wonderful mix of people there, too, though I don't know some of the names which would be recognised by those a lot younger than me. I remember telling Andy Puttock at the end of one day, that I was sorry for one of the Guns who must be going through a really bad time. He obviously wasn't doing very well. Andy looked a bit confused, and I told him I'd heard several times that this bloke was in dire straits. Andy then enlightened me: he was Mark Knopfler – of Dire Straits!

Another time there was a red-haired singer there from a strange-sounding band I misheard called Simply Dead – instead of Simply Red! It was Mick Hucknall. And people think it's funny that I asked this quiet bloke – a charming chap – what he did for a job: it was Eric Clapton!

Ian Botham is a regular there, too, and the first time I met him, he came up to me, and said: 'I've waited years to meet the legend!' I turned round to see whom he was talking about, and then realised that he was referring to me. He's broken all the records, and deserves the title 'legend', and he was referring to me!

I met Norman Marshall with Basil Kinch, at Farmington, in the 1970s. Basil asked me if I'd look after him, as he hadn't done much shooting. He turned up in a Ferrari, with a black pinstripe suit on, black shoes, and when Basil told me this was Norman, I said: 'Has he come to watch?' Basil said he'd come to shoot, but warned that he didn't know how experienced he was, as he'd had to borrow a gun. At the first drive, we were shooting near the boundary, and Basil said that any pheasants going back that way, were to be shot. He told me to take Norman with me.

Well, some of the birds were running out of the cover crop, and heading back home past us, and Norman started blazing away at them, almost on the ground. He wasn't hitting many, and I suggested that he should shoot at them up in the air, but he insisted we had to shoot everything! After the drive, I was very diplomatic, but ran him through the etiquette of shooting pheasants, and from that day on, we were great friends.

Pictured at Steve Thomas's excellent Prescombe shoot in good company – also present were Olympic and World champions Richard Faulds and George Digweed, along with Sir Ian Botham, his son Liam and two grandsons. (Photograph: Jake Eastham)

In those days we called him 'Pinstripe' as he always used to have come from a meeting before he went shooting. As time's gone on, he became 'The Silver Fox' or just 'Foxy'. I've had some great days with him, both shooting and fishing. He's been taking a couple of days from Andrew Witham at Bleasdale for years now, and that's a great shoot.

He has a shoot at his home as well, in Surrey. I helped a bit to set it up, suggesting where he might put down his cover crops, to take advantage of the rolling topography. There's one drive now called The Strip and I could see that if birds came off there, they would test the best, so he put 10 acres of cover up there. The next year there were Guns like Basil Kinch and Bill Joyce there, and even they couldn't touch the partridges coming over. 'I told you they'd miss 'em!' I said to Norman.

He was shooting at Shawford one day, and the last drive of the day we drove the teal off one of the lakes. In the gloom, Norman killed a passing blackbird. We didn't say anything, but at dinner afterwards, we announced there was 'a very special delicacy for Mr Marshall', and brought out a silver tureen with the blackbird on it.

I was shooting with Norman on what he calls his 'Boys' Day'. There are always a lot of birds, and, on the first drive, I was being pretty selective, and waiting for a really good one to try for. Then, of course, when a real high one came over, I missed it! My neighbour, who was shooting at everything, came up to me at the end of the drive, and – only half-jokingly – told me I needed to sharpen up.

On the second drive, the pheasants were crossing me, towards my neighbour, and I killed a stack of them. There were dead pheasants all around him, and he spent the drive dodging them. Clarky, who was on the other side of him, kept calling out: 'Is Fussell sharpening up now?'

Norman's a rogue for pulling legs. Once when we were fishing the Moy, I'd just got my first mobile phone, and he got one of his secretaries to ring me up, and she said she wanted to meet me. She said she'd come to my room that night. She kept ringing, and the messages got more and more fruity as the day went on. That night, I was so worried that I decided to push the wardrobe across the door, so that I wouldn't be disturbed, but the next morning I couldn't push it back! It took ages to get out, and everyone else was having a good giggle about it.

Norman arranged all the champagne for my 70th birthday party – mind you, I paid for it! We had 500 guests altogether, and we drank 180 magnums – it was some do! I was pretty tipsy, and standing on my head. A couple of local farmers bet me I couldn't do it, but I could. I was still pretty fit at 70.

Taking a high bird whilst seated at Bleasdale 2013 – the fore-end had fallen off my old Browning, but duct tape saved the day! (Photograph: Adrian Blundell)

I haven't fallen out with many people over the years. It has happened occasionally. Howard Bennett took a day at Cholderton, near Amesbury: a lovely shoot, and great for pigeons, which I shot there for many years. There was a resident syndicate – all wild birds, before it was then let, and a lot of pheasants put down. We were there in early November, and the pheasants had no tails. They'd obviously been let out late, and they shouldn't have been shot at all. The shoot tenant – and his son – stood as back Guns, and were shooting these poults that the front Guns were leaving. I went up to him, and told him in no uncertain terms that he was no sportsman if he shot birds like that.

The same man was once shooting on one of Charles Church's days, and I was two Guns down from him, with Susie Church between us. He started shooting Susie's birds, right across in front of her. After the drive, I asked Churchy why he'd invited the bugger, if he couldn't behave himself. Churchy didn't know what I meant, so I told him he'd been poaching Susie's birds.

We weren't numbering, and on the next drive Churchy placed me next to the poacher, and I deliberately shot about 20 birds that were heading straight for him, and they rained down around him. At the end of the drive, he came up to me, and berated me for shooting his birds. I told him that he clearly hadn't thought the same on the previous drive, when he'd shot all of Susie's birds. We hardly ever spoke after that.

Odd people have tried to poach my birds over the years: I put up with it for a while, but if they keep doing it, I return the compliment – and they soon get the message!

I had a real set-to once, with Ken Raines when we were shooting at Chilmark. It was hailing heavily, and we'd worked really hard to get a lot of partridges, and wild pheasants, into this field of roots. It was cold, and Ken was wearing a coat with a big hood, which he'd raised, to protect himself from the weather. Birds were going over the middle of the line, and they weren't getting shot at. I stopped the line, and went to see what was going on, and realised that Ken just couldn't see them. I tore him off a real strip, telling him that we'd worked bloody hard to get the birds there, and that he could f**k off home if he wasn't going to shoot them! He was very apologetic.

CHAPTER 12

CHURCHY

Charles Church ran a very successful house building company in the 1970s and '80s, pioneering many new techniques, and quickly gaining a reputation for upmarket quality homes. He took his company public in 1988, but suffered the hangover from the crash of October 1987, and bought back all the shares the following year.

He worked hard, and played hard, too, throwing enormous energy into whatever he did – as can be seen from his approach to the sport of shooting.

His other passion was vintage planes, which he restored at his Hampshire estate, Roundwood. He was at the controls of his beloved Spitfire Mark V on July 1st 1989 when it developed engine trouble, and he died in the crash which followed.

Charles Church deserves a chapter to himself: I first met 'Churchy' – as I got to call him – through a chap called Ted Gibbs, who knew John Steeds, a cricketing friend of mine who farmed near Bruton. Ted told me he'd met a man who was mad on

The 'A-Team' at Roundwood. From left: Churchy, Stephen Potter, Robin Pardoe, Brian Mears, PF, George Perry, John Long, John Davis (Photograph: Soot Potter)

shooting, and he'd like to meet me. He was a complete novice, and wanted me to teach him to shoot. I didn't think I could help him, but he kept ringing me up: he was very persistent.

I told him that I didn't think I could help him but he said 'You'll have to!' He was a very dominant personality. He kept driving down here: you could hear him coming, as he had a habit of a nervous whistle as he walked along, and his car would draw up, and the whistling would start, and my missus would say 'That man's here again!', and I'd almost run into the other room. He told me he was going to take some shooting, and told me I had to come. I'd heard all this before, but he meant it.

I told him that he couldn't become a good Shot without practice, so he started going to David Olive's Apsley Shooting Ground. David used to ring me and say 'He's had 500 shots, and he wants another 500 – he says he wants to shoot like Fussell does!'

After a couple of years, Churchy started making a lot of money, and he took over a shoot at Minal, north of Marlborough. I'd known it before: it was a good Wiltshire downland shoot – nothing special, but a good shoot to start off with. He got six of us together who'd shot with him for a couple of seasons, and we were all mates, and he called us 'The A-Team'. It didn't cost us anything: he was mad on shooting, and he paid for everything! The first season, he asked my advice on how many birds to put down, and I suggested that 5,000 would be a sensible start, to see how things went. I knew he'd do what he wanted anyway, and the next I heard from the keeper, was that there were 10,000 pheasants coming, and 5,000 English partridge! Of course the partridges didn't hang around, and we hardly shot any.

Susie wrote a song about each of us in the 'A-Team' at the time. Mine was sung to the tune of '*The Man who Broke the Bank at Monte Carlo*':

> *He walks along the Marborough Downs*
> *With an independent air.*
> *He'll give you such a stare,*
> *If you ever dare*
> *To miss a fox*
> *Or January cocks.*
> *You'll hear him sigh*
> *As he wipes your eye:*
> *It's 'Ferret Eyes Fussell'*
> *The Grand Old man of Minal!*

He lived in Dorset at the time, but he bought Roundwood, an estate between Andover and Basingstoke, and eventually moved there. He rang and told me about the purchase, saying it would be marvellous for pigeon shooting. I said I'd come up and have a look, and he was right: it was a wonderful place for pigeons – just north of Archie Coats' patch around Micheldever – there were 1,000s there, and in those days, they hadn't been shot at much: there just wasn't the pressure on them that there is now.

The first day I went up there, Churchy was there with his two brothers-in-law, and they had hardly ever shot a pigeon between them. I told them they just needed to spread out, and shoot what they could. I went to a spot where there seemed to be a bit of a flightline, and started to do rather well, and ended up with over 300. At the end of that first day, the other three had about 10 between them!

During the day, the gardener – Cook by name, and a bit of a rogue by nature – had come to see how I was getting on, and I told him it was a great spot, but my shooting was limited by a large oak tree on my right, which prevented me shooting much on that side. I couldn't believe it, but the next week when I went back, the oak tree had been cut down!

With Churchy and my spaniel Whisky at Minal. My hat was quite new then

That was the start of it, and I used to go up there most Saturdays to shoot pigeons, and I killed thousands there over the years. One day, Churchy said to me: 'I've been reading about pigeon towers', and I told him there was no way I'd go up one of those, and he replied: 'Well, I'm going to have some built.' The north end of Laverstoke Wood was the perfect place – a 25-acre mix of fir, and beech saplings – with the prevailing wind channelling the birds in huge numbers. We chose the positions for two towers, but I repeated that I wouldn't go up in one. A few weeks later, he rang and said he'd killed over 100 from one of the towers, and that I must try it. 'Come tomorrow!' he said, but I managed to persuade him to leave it a week to let the birds settle down.

The towers were built from scaffolding, and attached to two fir trees, which was fine until the wind started blowing, when they would sway. They had seats in them, and you had to try and position yourself to take account of the movement. There was a ladder, with a rope beside it, which you had to climb up.

I had a dog called Snipe at the time, and she couldn't work out where I was, but she soon got the hang of it, and collected up all the dead pigeons under the tower.

She did have problems with the odd bird which was wounded, and walking off, but she grabbed them, and put a paw on them to hold them down. The problem was when there were two or three of them, and she didn't know which one to hold down!

Churchy was in the other tower, and we were using walkie-talkies for the first time, and he kept asking me how I was doing. I replied that I was doing ok, but that the dog was knackered! He told me that I needed to kill the birds, not wound them; I responded that if he could kill any of the birds I was shooting at, he'd be doing all right too.

It reminded me of shooting rockdoves out of a boat, which I once did up in Scotland, in Crosskirk Bay. There were thousands of them, flying inland, skimming over the waves, and when they got about 100 yards from the cliffs they'd fly up almost vertically into roosts in the cliffs. As they'd never been shot at before, I reckoned I could have a good shoot, if I was in a boat, with a ghillie to row, and try and keep it in the same place. I killed about 150, and Jack, the old ghillie, had a landing-net, and we'd scoop them out of the sea. They'd come in really low, and then take off like snipe to get up the cliffs. Jack was more intent on picking them up, than keeping the boat steady, and when he was moving about, too, it made it almost impossible.

The 'A-Team' used to have a pre-season warm-up at Roundwood, and Churchy got us all there, and we had a marvellous lunch, with copious amounts of champagne. After lunch, Churchy said I was going to give a demonstration of how to shoot the clays off the high tower he'd built. Cooky was trapper, and the first clay came off, and I fired two barrels at it... and missed! The same thing happened to the second... and the third. I never normally missed those, and I missed about 10 in a row. The rest of the team were loving it.

Churchy said: 'I'll have a go!' and promptly broke two clays. 'That's how you do it, Phil!' I began to get suspicious, and Cooky shouted down: 'I'll send over a couple of proper ones now!', and I broke the next two. Churchy had had made some aluminium clays which were unbreakable!

One day when I was shooting with him, I noticed a bloke with a camera, who kept taking pictures of me. I asked Churchy who he was, and he just said he was an amateur photographer, who was interested in shooting. I thought little more about it, until one day Churchy phoned me up, and said that I must come up to Roundwood, as he now had me 'in steel', and we'd crack a bottle of champagne. I didn't know what he was talking about, until he handed me a Beretta SO3 EELL he had commissioned. On one of the locks, Beretta's master engraver, Giovanelli, had depicted me shooting pigeons. He really caught me, and I'm even wearing my favourite hat. Churchy wanted the same guns I had, and with me on one of them, as he thought it would help him shoot as well as me! I tried to tell him that just having the best gun wouldn't make him the best Shot, but he wouldn't have it. It was the same with cars: I went with him once in his Ferrari, and afterwards told him 'Never again!'

Churchy soon took on more shooting – names that are now renowned as classic pheasant shoots: Chargot, Miltons, Molland. Of course there wasn't the emphasis on high birds then that there is today, but these shoots followed the lead of David Hitchings at Gurston Down, in using topography to show birds at extremely sporting range. He had 13 keepers at one point, and all we had to do was tip the keeper; Churchy paid for everything else, including the accommodation. Incredible generosity.

I'd shot at Miltons before Churchy took it on. Coincidentally, it was run by a chap called Alan Milton, and Bill Joyce had suggested I went there if I wanted to see some really high pheasants. I'd introduced Bill to Gurston Down, but he said that the birds at Miltons were even more challenging – and he was right. The first time I went there, I found them very difficult, and it soon got round the shooting world that even I had struggled.

I remember the first time I shot with Churchy at Chargot. I knew the keeper there, Nick Boniface, as he'd come down from Wiltshire – he'd loaded for me when we shot at Miltons. I don't generally like a loader, as I don't like anyone looking over my shoulder, and I prefer to shoot at my own pace. Anyway, we got to chatting, and I discovered he'd started out just down the road from me here, near Melksham. I don't remember the name of the drive, but about 1,000 birds came out from this game cover on the top of a hill, and, naturally, headed back to their pen. Unfortunately, the pen was right behind Number 8, so Numbers 6,7, and 8 all got lots of shooting, but Churchy and I were in the middle of the line, and didn't get much. After the drive, Churchy asked me what I thought, and I said: 'The pen's in the wrong place. The essence of pheasant shooting is to feed them out, and fly them home – preferably over the middle of the line.' When the keepers were gathered together, Churchy said loudly: 'Mr. Fussell says that the pen's in the wrong place!' They looked at me as if I was the devil, but, the next season, that pen had been moved.

On another occasion, soon after he took it over, Churchy, Nick Boniface and I were walking round, and there was this cliff-face, and Church wanted to know if Nick could get pheasants to fly off the top of it. It was agreed that with a pen in the right place, and some cover the birds could be fed into, it was possible (it's now known as Spitfire, after Churchy's other passion). The following year, we tried the drive, and Churchy was adamant that he and I would stand right in the bottom of the valley, with the other Guns up the hillside in front of us. I protested that it would be impossible to hit anything at the height the birds were likely to be, and so it proved. We fired 1,800 shots on that drive, and I could honestly say that I didn't even hit, let alone kill, one bird! I told Churchy I'd never do the drive again, from that position, as it was plain stupid.

Marion, Alan Milton's wife, had been picking up a long way back, and came up to me, and said 'Phillip, I've got six of your birds', showing me the six hens she was carrying. I knew I hadn't killed anything, and asked for a brace of those birds to be put aside for me at the end of the day. When I plucked them, there wasn't a pellet mark on them; the dogs had pegged the tired birds when they landed.

Often, Churchy would ring me up, and say: 'We're off tomorrow; you must come!', and I'd say I couldn't, because I had work to do. 'I'll cancel it if you don't come!' Churchy would say, so I'd go. My missus used to say 'That bloody builder will be the death of you, you know.' I always tried to get home every night, but one day he rang, and said 'We're off to Scotland, grouse shooting at Drynachan (the Cawdor estate near Nairn).' And I asked 'How long for?', and Churchy replied that it would be for a week, and he'd also taken the fishing on the Findhorn, just for me. He'd actually bought 500 brace of grouse over four days shooting, and we shot those in three days. I was happy, as I could go fishing, and the rest of the team nominated me to talk to Churchy, and tell him what a wonderful three days we'd had, and not to worry about the fourth.

He exploded: 'I haven't invited you up here to go bloody fishing! We're having another day!' and we killed 280 brace the next day, of which I shot 103 birds. I had a local loader, and I couldn't understand a word he said. The last drive was a return drive, with the wind, and the grouse were coming in 20s and 30s, round this knoll, down a little valley, and I got a lot of shooting, and I was nailing them. I realised my loader was saying: 'Fooking 'ell! Fooking 'ell!' as I shot, and I turned to him and said: 'Just stick them in, Sandy, I understand you now!'

During that drive it had started to rain, quite heavily, and it looked as though the river might be quite good in a couple of hours, and I told Churchy that I wanted to have a go. He said that as long as I was back for dinner at 8.30, I could fish all I liked. I caught six salmon on the fly: the biggest 18½ lbs, and the smallest 9lb. It was getting late, so I hurried back to the hotel, dripping wet, to find everyone dressed up, and ready to go in to dinner. I knew they wouldn't believe what I'd caught, so I'd laid out the salmon in a row, in the back of my old Subaru, and – sure enough – they all trooped out to see them. What a day! – 103 grouse, and 6 salmon: I didn't think anything of it then.

I remember the hotel though, as one night they served us some of the grouse we'd shot. They were virtually raw! I just couldn't eat them, and had to ask for them to be cooked some more. I like most of my game well done: it won't dry out if it's properly cooked.

One spring, I'd penned up 300 hens on my laying field, and Churchy rang me up, and asked what I was doing. I said I was out haymaking, and he asked in which field, as he was going to be passing in his Spitfire. I told him where we'd be, but he came over head-high – hedge-hopping, real kamikaze stuff – straight over the laying pen, and, of course, the pheasants went wild.

I picked up a dozen dead hens in that pen, and I rang Churchy, and said: 'You bastard! Do you realise what you've done? You've ruined my egg production, and you've killed my pheasants!' He was very apologetic, and said that he'd get me 10,000 eggs from the local game farm. He also said: 'I didn't disturb the tractor, did I? I'll get you another one!' When the game farmer rang to ask about delivery of the eggs, I told him not to bother, but Churchy would have paid up.

There was a squash court at Roundwood, and when we were shooting one day, Churchy's financial adviser – who was called King – asked me if I played squash, and would I like a game after the shoot? I'd played 'Fives' at school, but didn't start playing squash till I was 50, but quickly got addicted to the game, and played all I could, to a reasonable standard. Churchy said I must play Kingy, so I borrowed a racket, and played in my pants, having removed my trousers. Kingy was all dressed up in sports gear, and I said before I had a bet on the match, I needed a bit of a knock-up first, as I hadn't played for a while. Well, I could quickly see that he hadn't a hope: he was crashing into the wall, and hitting the floor, so I said: 'What are we having on this match? I'll give you five points a game!' 'Five points!' said Kingy, 'I'll have some of that. Let's have £20 on it.' I said: 'That's a lot, but seeing as it's you, let's make it £30!' He didn't get a point!

I shot with Churchy all through the 1980s; he didn't really like going to other shoots: he just wanted to shoot with the 'A-Team'. He really lived life in the fast lane, and he was a great character, and a great mate. When he died, his wife Susie desperately wanted to keep the shoot at Roundwood going, so I helped her run that for the next three years. Cooky was the keeper: he understood the countryside, and ran the shoot well, but it was never the same after he left.

It was Churchy who gave me my hat. I'd had a particularly good drive one day with the 'A-Team', and someone swiped my hat and threw it in the air. The rest of the team fired at it, and blew it to bits, so Churchy said he'd get me another one. It was made in Dublin, and I wear it every day I go gameshooting; not always when I'm pigeon shooting, as I'm worried it might get lost. It's a little the worse for wear now, and it's been down a couple of rivers. People wouldn't recognise me without that hat! I remember seeing a video of the crowd at a clay shoot – the FITASC event I won in Switzerland as a Veteran in 1989 – before the prize-giving, and you couldn't see me, but you could see my hat! My sons picked me out immediately. I wear it in Churchy's memory.

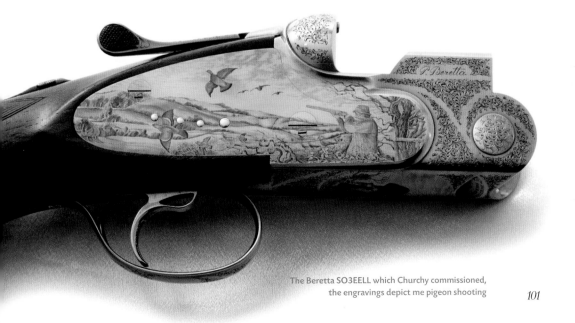

The Beretta SO3EELL which Churchy commissioned,
the engravings depict me pigeon shooting

CHAPTER 13

RYDON

In the 1980s I ran a lovely little shoot called Rydon, near Dunchideock, in Devon. Jane's sister, Tina, had moved there with her husband: it was a rough old farm, only about 125 acres of marginal land, but it had some wonderful steep-sided valleys.

They were struggling to make any money from it, and I went down there for tea one day with Jane, and, naturally, took the dog and gun, and went out to pot a few rabbits. There was a big estate nearby, which reared about 5,000 pheasants, and a few had obviously strayed. My dog put up a wonderful cock pheasant, high on the hillside, which flew right across above me, and sowed the seeds of an idea. I suggested to them that they had the potential for a fine little shoot, and that it could make them some money.

And so it turned out: on top of the farm, we managed to rent enough surrounding land to make seven drives. Lord Exmouth had some neighbouring land, and he'd also let us have lunch in his house occasionally, if we had a VIP team down. We had an American party, and they loved the razzamatazz with His Lordship. Even with the extra land, though, we only had enough drives to rest one per shoot, so we simply couldn't shoot any more often.

We had 730 laying hens at Shawford, and we picked up, on average about 12,000 eggs, which we sent to a game farm, and received 5,000 poults in return, which was the maximum possible we could release on the small acreage we had to play with. When they were released, we mixed aniseed into their wheat, and it certainly helped to stop them from straying. Cooky from Roundwood had given us the recipe: it was a mix of essence of aniseed and cooking oil, which we called 'Cooky's Hooch'!

We had a hell of a job getting the pens in – or my boys did! I told them where the posts had to be, and left them to it. The main pen was two acres of steep hillside, and each post had to be put in with a rammer. It took them months. The trees were full of half-inch long wood ants, too, which made the job even worse, as they'd fall down onto you, and give a hell of a sting.

Andrew and Titch really helped to get the shoot going. Titch wasn't that interested in shooting – he turned out to be a marvellous skier, and ski instructor – but Andrew lived and breathed the shoot. The following tale sums up their interest: we were plagued by a fox near the main release pen, which we just couldn't catch in a snare. I told the boys that they'd need to stake out the pen all day, and that the fox would come along, and they could shoot it. Andrew started, and was there from 4am until 8, when he went in for breakfast, and Titch took over. When Andrew went back at 10, he saw the fox, and realised it was ambling straight past where Titch was hidden…but no shot came, and the fox disappeared. When he went and asked Titch what had happened, he admitted he'd got bored, and taken the gun to pieces, but then he couldn't put it back together again when he saw the fox!

We planned 14 days – every Saturday – and charged £17.50 per bird for a planned 120 bird day. We always put plenty of birds over the Guns, and it was up to them how many they killed. We worked on the team of 10 Guns firing 600 shots – a 5:1 shot ratio – and we had some good teams, which shows how difficult these pheasants were. Often, they would only get 70 or 80 – one team shot 60, with nearly 1,200 shots – and the highest bag ever was 124. It wasn't just the height of the birds, but they were curling, too, which made them impossible for inexperienced Guns.

We held a practice day at the start, to try out the drives. Charles and Susie came, along with some Americans who had got in touch with me, and wanted to come and shoot over here. One of them had been very interested by my use of choked barrels, and he would phone me up and talk for hours about chokes, cartridges, and ballistics. When he turned up, he had bought a pair of Purdeys with full chokes. Unfortunately he was completely unable to hit anything with them! They all turned up, immaculately turned out, but were useless – not bad to have on a practice day.

The shoot quickly got such a reputation that we were always oversubscribed. It was so small that you couldn't shoot it more than once a week. People were offering wads of cash for a day there. One old friend – I shan't name him – used to come to me, and say: 'I want three days!' and I'd say I couldn't guarantee it, and he'd stick his hand in his pocket, and come out with a huge wedge of cash, and say: 'Can you guarantee it now, Phil?' The notes looked like they were hot off the press!

One of the reasons we were so popular was that not only was the shooting spectacular, but so were the lunches. Jane and Tina would do them, and the Guns could choose what they wanted to eat. The favourite was roast duck, which was delicious. If the team was local to us in Somerset, we'd come back to Shawford and have a late meal here, so they didn't have far to drive home.

One of the teams was brought by Bernie Spencer, a very good Shot. He owned a business called Bernie's Autos, and he taught a lot of high profile names in the music world to shoot, and also several West Country rugby stars.

George [Digweed] came down, early in his shooting career, when he hadn't really had any experience of really high pheasants. I don't think he fired a shot on the first drive, although four lovely pheasants soared over him, but he never raised his gun. After the drive, I went up to him, and asked

Well presented pheasants
(Photograph: Simon Everett)

him how he'd got on, and he replied that he hadn't had a bird over him. I told him he had to look up, not forward, as, even with his amazing eyesight, he simply hadn't been aware of the pheasants – they were that high.

We had to make the drives flexible, so that some teams could get a few birds in the bag, if they simply couldn't get on with the highest ones. The first drive was just a warm-up, as we never managed to get much cover on some awful land where the flushing point was. We had to put fir tops there as artificial cover to hold the birds.

The second drive was the best of the day: we had about six acres of kale on the top of the valley. There could easily be 400 or 500 pheasants in there. This was where I had to keep in communication with Andrew, who was running the beating line. He was then a student at agricultural college, and he used to bring his mates down for the day as beaters. Their girlfriends often came, too. We never knew quite how many beaters we'd have, but, unlike some shoots, the beaters seemed to have as much fun as the Guns did, and there was no segregation. Andrew was always really nervous, wanting to give the Guns a good day, as most of them were old friends of ours.

He would be in the middle of the line, so he could manoeuvre the beaters to put birds evenly over the line. Often, though, I'd tell Andrew halfway through the drive that he'd have to pull out, as they'd shot their quota. There might still be several hundred birds in the kale, and, on more than one occasion, after the horn had gone and the beaters were pulling out, there would be an almighty flush.

This led to one of the funniest incidents on the shoot. By now, everyone who came to shoot, knew that the second drive was the best, and they decided to try and stop me bringing it to a premature halt. They'd fed me several drinks after the first drive, and, when I decided to stop the second, I told Andrew that he should pull out when I blew the horn. I put it to my lips, and blew…and blew…but no sound came out. A sausage roll had been stuffed down the horn, rendering it useless! So Andrew kept going, and the Guns kept shooting, and I got redder and redder in the face. After the drive, the Guns were in tears.

Another day, a well-known clay pigeon Shot came down. Let's call him John! He greeted me with the news that he'd been shooting the day before at Ashcombe, the Devon high pheasant shoot, and he hadn't missed a bird, and that he was looking forward to shooting at Rydon as he'd heard the birds were very good.

He was Number 8 on the first drive, at the end of the valley, and he never fired a shot. As he walked back past me, he said he hoped there were more birds on the second drive. I said that he was going to Number 3, and there should be some good birds there. He asked me where the birds were coming from, and I pointed at an oak tree on the top of the hill in front of him, saying that they would come on a line from the oak tree, and follow the hedge line across the valley: 'They're quite nice pheasants.' I asked Andrew how things were looking, and he said there were a lot of birds up there. I replied: 'That's all I need to know!'

At that moment, an old cock pheasant got up, right from the back of the drive, cleared the oak tree, and soared across the valley over Number 3. It must have been 55 yards up. Up went John's gun: Bang! Bang! Nothing! Not even a feather. The next six birds which went over him produced the same result: Bang! Bang! Nothing! I edged up towards him, and he saw me and called: 'Where am I, Phil? Where am I?' I replied: 'John, you're at Rydon, and you haven't hit f**k all yet!'

There was an old pumphouse down behind the gunline, and we used to put a backgun there. Andrew remembers seeing two hen pheasants get up halfway through the drive, and rise another 10 yards above the usual flightline. All the beaters stopped to watch these two birds, which were agreed to be virtually out of shot. There was a flurry of shots from the front line, and neither bird was touched. A couple of seconds later, a shot was heard, and the first hen put her head back, and started to fall. Another shot, and the second was killed, and they plummeted down together. It was the best right and left I've ever seen. It was Ian Coley on the Pumphouse peg, and he remembers it to this day, too: 'Most of the regulars got to realise that the second drive of the day was always the big one, and that Number 3 was always the best peg. To get there, a Gun had to draw 10 for the first drive. We always had the cards on a silver tray, and they were stood up in such a way that Terry Clark realised that if he was sitting down, when he took his card, he could see the card's number, reflected in the tray. We never figured out how he always seemed to manage to pick Number 10 for the first drive – or, if someone had managed to get that card before he drew, then Number 1, or Number 9. It wasn't until after the shoot had closed, that he let on, the clever rogue!'

We rented a wood on an adjoining farm from a miserable bugger who I won't name, but we lost a lot of birds into it, and needed to drive it occasionally, to get them back. After one shoot, we decided that we needed to drive it the following week, so I left it to my brother-in-law, Ian, to talk to the owner, and just to confirm it was okay to do so. The following Saturday, Ian said that he couldn't get hold of the farmer, but he'd told his wife what we were planning, and that it should be okay.

We started driving the wood out as our third drive. It was on a steep bank, and the Guns lined out along the bottom. The drive started well, with plenty of pheasants being flushed, but then our neighbour turned up, and started raising merry hell! He asked us what the hell we thought we were doing in his wood, told us in no uncertain terms that we

Ian Coley remembers the Pumphouse peg to this day

hadn't spoken to his wife, and that we were trespassing, and that we should bugger off. So we did! I stopped the drive, and told the Guns what had happened. At the end of the day, I apologised to Ginger Chatfield, who'd taken the day, and gave him a £500 refund out of embarrassment, as we'd had to pull one of the drives, and they'd only ended up with about 70 birds, despite firing a lot of shots.

A friend of Andrew's, Andy Wolsey, did the keepering for us. He'd been a van delivery driver, but was bored with it. So he lived in a tiny caravan at the farm, and spent all his pay in the local pub. I used to have to settle his tab at the pub, before he got anything that was left – and there often wasn't any! He got paid a small amount, but got all the tips from the shoot. He loved it. He'd carry a gun on shoot days, and act as stop, and shoot any foxes that came out. His main job was dogging-in, which was essential on such a small acreage.

We didn't drive anywhere: there weren't any real tracks, so from the farmhouse we walked out, Guns and beaters, and never used a vehicle the whole day. It was lucky the beaters were young and fit, as they had a hard day.

My old cricketing friend, Mike Taylor, came and picked up for us – he hardly missed a day. He used to have The Wheatsheaf at Combe Hay, just outside Bath, and he liked a drink. He trained dogs as well, and liked to demonstrate their prowess. One evening he wanted to show how good this new dog was, so he got a pigeon – in the feather – and chucked it into the restaurant. It landed on a table, where two diners were enjoying their meal. The dog went into the restaurant, and gently retrieved the pigeon from the table. 'What a dog!' was all he said.

I took Mike out pigeon shooting – he'd never been before, and knew nothing. It was a big field, which I had shot often over the years, and it had two bushes on a fenceline where hides could be placed, about 400 yards apart. I asked him which of two bushes he'd like to shoot from, and he happened to choose the one furthest from Great Ridge, where the birds were coming from. I put out some decoys for him, and then set up myself. He killed two, and I had 280. He said: 'Every time I saw anything coming, it was heading straight for me, but then it saw your decoys and went to you!'

Sadly, we had to close the Rydon shoot in 1990, when the financial crisis forced Ian and Tina to sell the farm when interest rates went sky-high. People still talk about it, and say how good it was. Some of the best stories are unrepeatable!

Susie Church wrote another of her songs about the shoot. We used to sing it at the end of the day, after a lot of liquid lubrication! It was sung to the tune of *The 12 Days of Christmas*:

> *On the first day at Rydon, Philip Fussell said to me:*
> *'A wondrous shoot this will be'.*

> *On the second day at Rydon, Philip Fussell said to me:*
> *'Two days of fog,*
> *But a wondrous shoot this will be.'*

> *On the third day at Rydon, Philip Fussell said to me:*
> *'Three lame birds,*
> *Two days of fog*
> *But a wondrous shoot this will be.'*

> *On the fourth day at Rydon, Philip Fussell said to me:*
> *'Four bloody yanks,*
> *Three lame birds,*
> *Two days of fog*
> *But a wondrous shoot this will be.'*

> *On the fifth day at Rydon, Philip Fussell said to me:*
> *'Five blank drives,*
> *Four bloody yanks,*
> *Three lame birds,*

Two days of fog
But a wondrous shoot this will be.'

On the sixth day at Rydon, Philip Fussell said to me:
'Six beaters beating,
Five blank drives,
Four bloody yanks,
Three lame birds,
Two days of fog
But a wondrous shoot this will be.'

On the seventh day at Rydon, Philip Fussell said to me:
'Seven dogs a running,
Six beaters beating,
Five blank drives,
Four bloody yanks,
Three lame birds,
Two days of fog
But a wondrous shoot this will be.'

On the eighth day at Rydon, Philip Fussell said to me:
'Eight shooters missing,
Seven dogs a running,
Six beaters beating,
Five blank drives,
Four bloody yanks,
Three lame birds,
Two days of fog
But a wondrous shoot this will be.'

On the ninth day at Rydon, Philip Fussell said to me:
'Nine blackbirds over,
Eight shooters missing,
Seven dogs a running,
Six beaters beating,

Five blank drives,
Four bloody yanks,
Three lame birds,
Two days of fog
But a wondrous shoot this will be.'

On the tenth day at Rydon, Philip Fussell said to me:
'Ten locals staring,
Nine blackbirds over,
Eight shooters missing,
Seven dogs a running,
Six beaters beating,
Five blank drives,
Four bloody yanks,
Three lame birds,
Two days of fog
But a wondrous shoot this will be.'

On the eleventh day at Rydon, Philip Fussell said to me:
'Eleven foxes fleeing,
Ten locals staring,
Nine blackbirds over,
Eight shooters missing,
Seven dogs a running,
Six beaters beating,
Five blank drives,
Four bloody yanks,
Three lame birds,
Two days of fog
But a wondrous shoot this will be.'

On the twefth day at Rydon, Philip Fussell said to me:
'A double, and leave the bottle, please!'

CHAPTER 14

GEORGE DIGWEED MBE

George Digweed, who was awarded an MBE in 2009, is another who deserves a chapter to himself. My first recollection of George was at one of the major clay competitions; it must have been about 1985. I kept seeing this young chap, in the background, and he seemed to be following me around, and watching what I was doing. Eventually, I went up and asked him where he was from, and what he was doing, and he replied: 'I'm here to watch you.' I won that competition, and in the bar afterwards, he was still there, sitting, and watching. He had a gamebag on his back, and was wearing plus fours; I said: 'Still here, young man?' and he said: 'I'm not going home yet,' but he never had a drink.

After that, we met quite often, as I was doing quite a lot of clay pigeon shooting. He progressed pretty quickly, and it wasn't long before he won a major competition – and he beat me! So I wrote him a letter, congratulating him, and saying that I thought there would be many more to come. He must have been about 18 at the time.

From that date, we became good friends, but make no mistake, when

George Digweed MBE – the best (Photograph: Jake Eastham)

George is shooting, he's cut off from everything. His concentration is unbelievable. The pressure he's under: it's the same as a racing driver. I've never seen his equal, at clays or live game. Even the best when I was a kid – people like Joe Wheater – wouldn't stand a chance against George.

I told him when he started that the worst thing he would encounter was jealousy. A lot of people are jealous of George, and run him down. It's a competitive sport, and he's the best.

He's a good countryman, too, and a good keeper. He runs three shoots, and understands how to show a pheasant. He also likes pigeon shooting. He rang me up a few years ago, and said he had a keeper friend from up North, who'd never shot 100 pigeons, and could I help? I told him that, as he well knew, pigeon shooting was such an uncertain sport that I couldn't guarantee anything, but I'd do my best. It was March, and one of the farmers at Finkley had just drilled some spring barley, and I knew there were a few birds on it. I asked George how the keeper could shoot, and George said he was a fair Shot.

So I met them at Andover, and I put them both out where I thought the best places were, and the keeper shot 102. I was about a mile away – keeping the birds moving – and I phoned George, and asked him how he was getting on. He replied: 'Oh, I'm getting one or two, but they're not coming too well.' At the end of the day, I went to where he was, and there were birds everywhere. It looked like a snowstorm! We picked up over 400 around his hide. He said there had been a football match going on in a field about 200 or 300 yards away, and the ref had come over and asked him if he minded not shooting in an arc covering the playing field, as he was dropping shot on the centre-forward! I went back there three days later, and shot over 300 myself.

He's also pretty good at pheasants. I forget the name of the drive at Bleasdale, but these pheasants were coming off moorland, and looked like swallows. There was a strong wind, and the birds were drifting on it. George was number 5, and he killed about 20 pheasants, all at least 60 yards up, and they all dropped, with their heads back, stone dead. I was back gun behind him, and, halfway through the drive, he just turned round, and motioned with his arm that I should move along to a more productive position! I said: 'Don't worry, George, they're too good for me!' I've never seen anyone to touch him.

The drive before, though, he'd missed quite a lot. They were good pheasants, about 50 yards up, but he wasn't touching them. At the end of the drive, he came up to me, rather gingerly, and said 'You know, Phil, I brought out the wrong box of cartridges: I took them out of the gunroom, and I hadn't had them on the central heating.' I couldn't believe George was making excuses, but he told me to look down the barrels, and, sure enough, they were pretty dirty.

Anyway, he took new cartridges to the next drive, and, as I said, shot amazingly well. Andrew Witham always used to say that we weren't a bad team, 'but not as good as the Percy brothers' [Ralph, Duke of Northumberland and Lord James]. Of course this got George going, and, after one drive there, when we'd all shot pretty well, he went up to Andrew, and said 'I don't suppose the Percy brothers were watching, were they?!' He's pretty competitive, but then he wouldn't have won all those World Championships without it.

I can still teach him a thing or two, though. At Bleasdale, he shot a very high rook, but he insisted it was a crow! I was next Gun, and told him it wasn't a crow, but a rook. George was insistent, so we had a bet of a bottle of whisky on it. It was the last drive of the day, so I sent one of the young keepers out to where the disputed

THE MASTER AND THE BOY
(BUT WHO'S WHO?)

Wellow Trekking Centre

FRANK AND JUDY SHELLARD
01225 834376

Coaching a very young George Digweed
(Photograph: Wellow Trekking Centre)

bird had fallen. George had a word with him as he went, and I guessed that he was telling him that if it was a rook, he wasn't to bring it back. I saw him pick the bird, but when he was about 100 yards away, he dropped it, and, when he got back he said he couldn't find it! I said: 'I've got eyes in my head!', and staggered up to where he'd dropped it, and brought back the rook. I did get my bottle of whisky!

I was shooting at Owley, one of George's shoots, in Kent, when he had a bit of a tiff with his neighbours, who were shooting the same day. When he gets mad, he shoots even better! He shot four pigeons stone dead that must have been well over 60 yards up. Then a jackdaw flew by – it must have been 100 yards away, and Bill Joyce said: 'He'll never get that.' But he did, again, stone dead. It was an amazing shot.

He came to shoot at Shawford, on one of the boys' days. He stood right at the back, in the third rank, on our duck drive, and fired 32 cartridges... for 32 ducks. If he misses, though, he'll give himself a good talking to: he wants to be perfect.

He's pretty handy with a rifle, too. He came down to Finkley once when we had a problem with the rabbits there. He had a silenced rifle, and a night sight. I drove, as I knew the ground, and he was on the back of the pick-up, with Cooky, the Roundwood keeper, who was there to help pick up the rabbits. He told me to stop when he tapped once on the cab roof, and move on when he tapped twice. All I heard was the tap, and then the 'Phut! Phut!' of the silenced .22. After a couple of hours, it came on to rain, and George said we'd have to stop as the rain was getting onto the scope.

Mind you, we couldn't have done much more, as the back of the pick-up was completely filled with dead rabbits, up to his knees. We only covered about 200 acres, but got 280 rabbits, and George said: 'I'll just paunch them!' He was a butcher, and you've never seen anyone paunch so quickly. He had a penknife with a blade as sharp as a razor, and he held this in his fingers about halfway down, so that it didn't go too far into the rabbit as he worked. Cooky would hand him a rabbit, he'd hold it between his legs and slice it open, and rip the guts out and throw them away – quicker than it takes to tell. It only took half an hour. We parked right by the railway embankment, and there were some blackthorn bushes there, and the guts got caught up in them.

A few days later I was up there pigeon shooting, and Ron, the keeper said: 'You shot some rabbits didn't you? You should have seen the magpies!' It hadn't taken long for the Andover magpies to find the gut-covered bushes, and feast on them.

CHAPTER 15

THE QUARRY

I've already written about rabbits, pigeons and partridges, as they played such a role in my early shooting years.

GROUSE

I haven't done a lot of grouse shooting, but the first time I went, it was to Wemmergill. At the Barnard Castle hotel that we stayed in, I'd seen a warning that the fine for shooting a greyhen was £5. I killed 13 grouse on the first drive, and as we lined them up on the butt, my loader said: 'You've shot a greyhen!' You know when you go over a hump-back bridge, and you get that awful feeling in your stomach? Well I had that feeling: I couldn't believe I'd shot a greyhen, and would have to pay £5, which was a lot of money then. I was almost shivering, but my loader said: 'Don't worry, I'll stick it down a rabbit hole!' which he did, and stamped down the soil around it. We stopped for a drink, and everyone was crowded round my butt, with their dogs, when two of the labs started digging at this rabbit hole. I was sweating, although the other Guns weren't taking any notice. The labs soon uncovered the evidence, but my loader just went and picked it up, and said: 'Must have been a stoat got that!' and pushed it back into the hole again.

It happened again, many years later. I was Bob Merrick's guest, and it was a windy day. I was next door to Robin Pardoe, and he was not shooting at his best. The grouse were drifting past me on the strong wind, and I was politely leaving them for Robin. I hardly had a shot until just before the horn went to stop shooting in front. About 20 grouse came round in front, missing me again, but there was one lone bird just behind them, and I killed it stone dead. It fell in Robin's butt!

At the end of the drive, I went to Robin, and he was upset at how badly he'd shot, and then he told me that the grouse which had landed in his butt was a greyhen! He said the fine was £500. I said: 'How much?!!!' Bob Merrick came up, and said that he hoped I'd got enough notes, but later relented, as he'd forgotten to mention the fine at the briefing.

I never found grouse that difficult, but I've never shot them late in the season. Shooting low, and quickly, at lots of pigeons, helps you to get onto grouse. I remember another time I was shooting with Bob Merrick, and his wife, Pauline, was with me. It was a return drive, with a short horizon. I knew I would have to be very quick, and anticipated where the grouse were likely to come, and where I would have to kill them.

My neighbour just looked relaxed – too relaxed. The first six grouse that came over him, he did manage to get a shot at... about 60 yards behind. I told Pauline that he wasn't going to shoot anything like that. I told her where I would shoot them... and I did. I had about 10 grouse down – shot in front – at the end of the drive. My neighbour couldn't believe it, and asked how I'd done it. I simply said that I'd anticipated where the birds were going to come from. He simply hadn't been ready for the birds in time.

PHEASANTS

When I started out gameshooting, I usually shot partridges, and, later, what I call Wiltshire pheasants. There weren't 'High Bird' shoots then. When you go out now, and there are people using 3s and 4s, because the birds are so high, I don't reckon that's sporting. I'd shoot birds out to 50 yards, with full choke, and they'd be dead. Now you see birds at 80 yards getting shot at, and flinching, but they're not dead. I don't see any point in shooting pheasants where there's an element of luck. Having said that, I can't see how George [Digweed] does it so consistently. I use the same cartridges as him, but I'll never shoot like him.

The other side of it is that too many Guns now don't pick out the good birds: they shoot the easy ones in a flush. I still try and pick out a nice bird. They pick out the ordinary ones you could kill with a catapult!

It was in the early '70s when high pheasant shooting, as we now know it, started to be developed. David Hitchings at Gurston Down was one of the first to use the topography of the Wiltshire downland to show high birds. I first shot there in 1973 as Ken Raines's guest, and then was a member of the syndicate David ran, for several years.

One of the highest drives at Gurston is called Rowberry, and one day, I was between the Potter brothers who were well-known Wiltshire Shots, and very good they were, too. I shot at a hen pheasant, and – it was just luck, as it was so high – it floated down and landed about 10 yards in front of me. It had clearly been stunned by a pellet, but wasn't dead: as soon as it came down, it was walking round in circles.

While the drive continued, and the Potters were busy, I grabbed the pheasant, and wrung its neck. After the drive, they agreed that it was the highest pheasant they'd ever seen shot stone dead, while I knew that if it had stayed there another two minutes, it could have flown away!

After this shoot at Gurston on 21 November 1973, David Hitchings noted: 'Another great day with some very fine shooting, in particular Nigel Potter, Philip Fussell, and John Potter, put on such an exhibition of high pheasant shooting at Rowberry that I felt honoured to have been a witness of it. The three of them killed 29 pheasants between them, with no runners – they were all stone dead in the air.'

At West Molland in 1990 (Photograph: Soot Potter)

It's wonderful how certain drives, and certain shots stick in the mind after all these years. I remember a pheasant day at Lodge Farm. We were doing a drive called Moss Hill, and they blanked out a wood into a field of kale on the top of the hill, and we counted 114 pheasants going into the drive. There were six of us shooting, and one beater went into the kale and started flushing the birds. Not one got back to the wood, and we killed 114 pheasants on that drive!

Andy Puttock remembered watching this drive from the beating line, with the keeper, Bob Acheson. 109 birds had been flushed, and killed, and the last five birds rose together. Bob said: 'At least one of these poor buggers will get away!' He hadn't reckoned on Philip killing the first bird about 50 yards out, and then reloading the one barrel, and killing another two. His neighbour, Bob Browning, then polished off the two survivors. Bob A went over to his boss, Colin Matthews, and said: 'You don't call this sport, do you? It's f**king murder!'

One of the most difficult shots is the high gliding pheasant, because it's so difficult to judge its speed. I remember one at Tetton only last year. It was the end of a drive, and the horn had gone, when a hen got up right from the back of the cover, and headed directly for me. It must have been 70 yards up, and I thought: 'Well, I'll just have a go at that', even though I really thought it was out of shot. I must have caught her with one pellet under the chin, as she folded up in mid-air. My young friend, Toby Bennett, was standing beside me, and I won't record what he said!

That was last year; this one must have been 50 years ago, when we were shooting at Coombe Farm, the Hillyers' shoot, near Sherborne. I was a bit in need of a haircut at the time, and not looking my neatest. Bob told me to go and stand by a water trough on the second drive. When I asked him why, he said, that there were some good pheasants on the drive, and the best of them always seemed to fly over that particular trough. There was a stop called Ivor standing about 100 yards past me, for the next drive.

No sooner had the drive started, than a hen pheasant got up, climbing and turning on the wind, and headed straight over me by the trough. It was probably 45-50 yards up – but don't forget we all used 7 shot for pheasants in those days. Several Guns fired at her, but missed, but I absolutely folded her up, and she landed way down the valley. While we were having drinks afterwards, Bob asked Ivor if he'd seen who shot the high hen, and Ivor replied, pointing at me: 'That thar girt rough bugger!'

Looking back, the high pheasants I remember have mostly been hens. It seems that individual birds tend to be hens, and they stick in the memory. I think perhaps they fly slower than cocks, though, so are easier to kill.

Bill Joyce remembered driving round Church Farm with Philip a few years ago, and Philip pulled up in a gateway. After a few seconds, he said: 'Are you thinking what I'm thinking: about that cock pheasant?' Bill admitted he had been thinking about the same bird, which had appeared on a shoot when he was beating, as a boy, in the 1950s. Philip had been walking with the beaters, and the cock had got up, and curled back on the wind. Needless to say, Philip despatched it cleanly with one shot, but the event had stuck in both minds for 60 years.

I was shooting at Molland once, and I hit a high hen pheasant very hard. She planed down a long way and hit the ground by a river a good 200 yards behind the line. I've always been keen that any wounded birds are picked up, and I checked with the pickers-up at the end of the drive. I wasn't convinced that they'd found her, so I sent my dog off. She was gone a long time, and eventually I could see her coming back with something in her mouth. It wasn't the hen, but a kelt (a salmon that has spawned)!

SNIPE

I've never been that keen on shooting woodcock. They are such a beautiful bird. I've shot a few on driven shoots, and I love to eat them. Snipe were a different matter, though. A gang of us used to go down to the Somerset Levels, near Stathe, to Bob Parker's Black Smock pub. It was all withy-beds round there then, grown for basket-making, and, when the water was right, the beds would be full of snipe. It had to be just squelchy underfoot – not too wet, and not too dry.

We'd drive one bed out – only using one beater – and watch where the wisps of snipe went, and then we'd move on to the next. They always fly off into, or across, the wind – never downwind. We'd often shoot 80 to 100 snipe in the day. One funny memory concerned Ken Raines, who was a big heavy-set man. To get around, you often had to cross the rhynes, or drainage ditches, and to do this, you used a pole to push yourself across. It was quite easy to do when you got the hang of it. Ken wasn't happy about this at all, and asked: 'How far round is it, if I can't get across?', but I told him it was too far. He wanted me to show him again, how to vault the rhyne, so I did, back and forth, until he got the courage to do it. He got halfway across, though, and stopped... and then slowly slid down the pole into the water. He was soaked to the skin. It was a devil of a job to get him out.

Sadly, there aren't the withy-beds now, so the snipe have gone.

VARIOUS

Howard Bennett took me to a shoot near Kings Somborne in Hampshire. On one drive I was Number 8. It was in a valley, with rough woodland on one side, which the beaters were walking through towards me. I was out of sight of the other Guns – slightly above them, and round a bit of a corner. I shot a few pheasants, and then a jay came along. It had obviously seen the line of Guns, and kept out of range in front of them, but it hadn't counted on me being where I was. It learned its lesson.

Then another one came, and another, and another... At the end of the drive the other Guns thought I must have a stack of pheasants there, and I told them to look by my peg. I'd laid out all 13 – yes 13! – jays which had flown to my peg.

STALKING

I only went stalking once. A couple of friends told me that I must try it, so I went. We were up at Dalmally, in Argyll, and we seemed to crawl for miles! I didn't really have the right kit on, so I was cold, wet, knackered and miserable. We were using .303 Lee Enfields, and we zeroed them in before going on the hill. I'm left-handed, which makes using the bolt difficult, but I shot all right at the dummy deer. Eventually, we found an 11 pointer, and I was allowed to shoot it. I poleaxed it, and told the ghillie: 'That's the first deer I've ever shot, and it will be the last one, too!' And it was. I brought the antlers home, and I hung them up on the side of the village house I was living in. They hung there, until the board they were mounted on, rotted.

People have asked me to shoot the roe deer here, but I just don't get it. I don't see the sport. If they charged at you, that would make it more exciting, but they just stand there, they are almost tame.

HUNTING

I used to love watching the Avon Vale hunt: watching the hounds work, and trying to second guess where the fox might go. After my riding accident as a child, I never wanted to get on a horse again, so I used to follow the field in my van. The Master, Neil Parker once said to me: 'Philip, I know you like your hunting, but invariably you're turning my fox. You're always parked where the fox wants to go!' I used to try and think like the fox, and try and think where he might go – and I was often right.

I rode to hounds once – quite by accident. I was watching the Old Berks in my

Renault van. A fox went to ground under the road, right by where I'd parked. All my mates were riding, and one, called Bosley, asked me to hold his horse, while he had a fag, as we waited for the terriermen to come up and bolt the fox. Bosley's horse had won at Cheltenham, but was now retired. He told me to jump on, and walk the horse round for a few minutes, which I did.

The next thing I knew, the fox had bolted, and hounds, riders, and Bosley's horse all charged after it. 'Hang on!' shouted Bosley, but I couldn't hold him, and off we went, over several jumps, and into the distance. Another friend, Jim Manners, was alongside, and he shouted over: 'What are you doing here, Phil?' I was in casual clothes, and in my Wellingtons: 'Don't ask me!' I shouted back, and it was at least couple of hours before I was very relieved to see Bosley in my van, and I could return his Cheltenham winner.

Even though I enjoyed hunting, I never had any qualms about shooting foxes. I've always regarded them as the wild gamebird's number one enemy. We were shooting once on George Perry's farm at Oakhill, on one side of the valley, and the Mendip Farmers were hunting on the other side. George had told the hunt we were shooting that day, and not to come onto the farm, which was quite small. Suddenly, though, a fox broke, and the hounds followed, right down through the line. I just couldn't kill it, as I knew all the hunt was watching. It ran past me, and in front of George Perry, who shot it stone dead. He was livid, and swearing at the hunt. I was with my son, Andrew, and we hid behind one of the cars, so that, hopefully the Master wouldn't see us.

CHAPTER 16

THE TOOLS OF THE TRADE — AND HOW TO USE THEM

Afterthe .410s I had in my youth, I used my father's 12 bore for some years. It was a Warrilow, made in Chippenham, which only intermittently worked in both barrels, so it wasn't ideal!

Much to my surprise, my father bought a 'Utility' Churchill 25. It was at the time when 25 inch barrels were the latest idea. He left it to me when he died, but I couldn't get on with it. I was then shooting a lot with John Florey, who was using a really old gun, and I suggested he had a go with the Churchill. He wore that gun out! He never paid me for it either, but I was using one of his 8 bores for wildfowling, and I hung on to that instead.

The first 12 bore I bought myself, was a Sauer – a German side-by-side – which I bought from Conyer's in Blandford for £45. It had a silver oval on the stock which was engraved Grand Prix Monte Carlo 1898. I shot everything with that – game, pigeons, and clays – it was a super gun. I used it when I was runner-up in the British Open. It was a close thing, though, as the previous week, I pulled the front trigger, and it just snapped off. I found it, and got Fred Cooper to braze it back on for me in time for the competition.

I used a side-by-side for all my gameshooting until the early '70s. If you turned up with an over-and-under on a game shoot, people looked at you as if you were carrying a machine-gun! This continued until so many clay shooters started shooting game, that over-and-unders gradually became accepted. My favourite side-by-side was a beautiful Boss.

How I came by it was quite a story: I knew a man called Frank Reedhead, who had taken the shooting at George Price's farm near Salisbury. He turned up one day with a new gun – a side-by-side Boss. It had belonged to the Shah of Iran, or someone like that. It was Number 5 of a set, but he didn't own the others. He asked me to guess how much it cost: I hadn't a clue, so I said £200. '£200! You must be joking', he exclaimed, 'I paid £1,400 for it!'

He told us to watch him shoot with his new gun. Lots of people think that buying an expensive gun will turn them into a good Shot. It's rubbish! Frank was like that: he banged away with this Boss, and couldn't hit a thing. The next week,

he tried again, with no success. 'Someone's been messing with this gun!' he said, so Fred Cooper – who knew quite a lot about guns, and liked tinkering with them – had a look at it. Fred winked at me, and said: 'It looks as if it's been recessed, Frank; they've buggered the pattern up.' So Frank said: 'I'm going to give it to young Fussell to try; we'll see if he can hit anything with it.'

So Frank gave me the gun, and said: 'If you can't shoot with it, there must be something wrong with it.' We went off to shoot some English partridges over a valley, and the first covey came over: Bang! Bang! I missed with both barrels. And the next, too – Bang! Bang! Not a feather.

I used a side-by-side until the early '70s

'I knew it!' said Frank. 'Fussell can't hit anything with it. There's something wrong with it.'

I said: 'I'll tell you what Frank: I'll give you a hundred quid for it.' He nearly exploded! 'I paid £1,400 for it, and won't sell it for less!' 'But there's something wrong with it, Frank,' I said, handing back the gun, and he tried it again: Bang! Bang! Nothing! He was so frustrated, that he said to me: 'You pay me £100 next Saturday, and the gun's yours.'

So I handed over the money, and the first covey of partridges came over, and Bang! Bang! Whack! Whack! I got a lovely right and left. I said: 'It seems to be working better now Frank!' He shouted: 'You young bugger! What have you done to that gun?'

In fact, the Boss had been messed around with. It had been rebarrelled by Hellis, and the chokes had been taken out. Fred Cooper said that when you cleaned it, you could feel there was no resistance as you pushed through the cleaning rod. He said we should pattern the open-choked Boss against the fully-choked Browning, and he couldn't believe the result: the Boss threw a better pattern. Fred said the barrels had been recessed, so they threw a tighter pattern, despite the lack of choke.

Ten years later, I had a set of Boss barrels made for it, choked ¾ and full, but they never threw as good a pattern as the old Hellis barrels. So, although I've always preferred tight chokes, those old barrels threw a deadly pattern, and I killed a lot of birds with them before I knew they had no apparent choke. Even after I got the new barrels, I'd sometimes use the old ones, just because I felt happier with them. I was so used to killing everything, that if I missed, I'd blame the gun!

I used that Boss for 20 years, until I moved on to an over-and-under, when they were more generally accepted. Then I went to a charity clay shoot, organised by Howard Bennett, at David Olive's Apsley Shooting Ground, where you had to use a side-by-side. I'd been using an over-and-under for some time, simply because of the amount of pigeon shooting I was doing, but I took the Boss, and I couldn't hit a thing with it. On the Tower, where I was usually pretty strong, I only hit half of them: I couldn't pick up the line with it. I got to the stage where I said: 'Well, as I can't hit anything with it, I might as well sell it!' A chap I knew from Dorset heard this, and said; 'How much do you want for it?' and I said I wouldn't let it go for less than five grand. I only said £5,000 because I didn't really want to sell it.

I said: 'You have it for next shooting season, and if you can't get on with it, I'll take it back and give you your money back.' We shook on that, and he took the

gun, but I never got paid! I didn't see him very often, and he never got in touch. I was shooting with Nelson Dance, and he asked me about the Boss, and I said I'd sold it, but had never been paid by this chap. He said 'We'll see about that.' He was quite an influence in the shooting world, and, within a week, a cheque for £5,000 arrived in the post. I never had the gun back, either, but I still miss it. It was the gun I really learned to shoot with, but when I was doing a lot of pigeon shooting, it was quite a light gun, and it kept getting scratched in the hide, so I moved on to a heavier over-and-under. I'd love to get it back.

I had a Holland & Holland, too. When Dutch Elm disease struck, a chap came to me and asked if he could take the elms, which I agreed to. We agreed a price, and he took quite a few, and then I asked for us to square up. He mumbled that times were tight, so I told him to stop taking any of the timber. At this, he mentioned that he had a Holland, and I told him to bring it over. It was an old gun, but worth a few bob, and I told him I'd take it in payment for the elms. Much later, when George [Digweed] persuaded me to try a Perazzi, and I decided I wanted a Perazzi MX12, I went into Greenfield's, the gunshop in Salisbury, and tried to do a deal with the Holland, and also a Watson side-by-side I had won. Eventually, they came back to me, and agreed a swap, with no money changing hands. I had the Perazzi made to match my favourite Beretta, and I virtually wore that gun out, too.

Hollands brought out a gun called The Sporter – an over-and-under game gun – and invited me to Haddeo to try one before the launch, as they said they'd like me to use one. I would have been happy to, if they'd given me one, but they wanted me to buy one – for over £20,000! They looked after me very well, and it was a great day's shooting, but I didn't buy one.

I also used a pair of Grant side-lever side-by-sides for a while: beautiful guns, but they had double triggers, and, having got used to single triggers, I'd always pull the front trigger twice! It was very frustrating – you should have heard the language – so they had to go.

When I had started shooting a lot of pigeons in the early '60s, I knew I needed more of a workhorse type of gun, and I was offered a Browning A1 by my cousin, John Hillier. It was the first over-and-under gun I'd ever used, and I paid £40 for it, second-hand. I used it everywhere, and one day I left it down by the piggery, as I was using it to kill crows that were coming for the pig food. The next time I went to get it, it had been stolen. I never told the police, but some time later, a local told me that he knew where my gun was. He wouldn't tell me who had taken it, but I offered him £10 if he got it back, and within a week I had it back.

By now, I'd bought a new Browning A1 from Fred Cooper for £65, as I was so taken by the one that had been stolen. I put thousands of rounds through that gun, and killed 1,000s of pigeons. I used to use it for wildfowl, too, and, when over-and-unders became more accepted, I used it for all my gameshooting, too. I've probably shot half a million pigeons with that gun!

I won quite a few guns in clay competitions. One I remember was a Bettinsoli, won at a big event at the Bath & West showground. They were the latest thing in guns at the time, but I couldn't get on with it – it had strange trigger pulls. I sold it, but didn't get much for it.

After my success in the World Championship in 1988, Beretta said they'd make me an SO best quality gun – free! I went to the Game Fair, to meet their top engraver, Giovanelli – who spoke no English – and Gunmark founder Bjorn Waktare. I wanted wildfowl on one lock, and partridges on the other. Giovanelli had bought some prints of both ducks, and partridges, that he intended to use, and on the partridge print, one of the covey had a leg down. I said I didn't want a bird with a leg down on my gun, but it was a hell of a job to make myself understood – and why it was so important! Eventually, I got a pencil and crossed out the hanging leg. I have to say the end result is superb, and the gun is beautiful. I used it for years, until, on George's recommendation, I started using Perazzis.

Now I'm back to a Beretta 20 bore, which is a bit easier on my poor shoulder, which is showing signs of extreme wear after all the thumps it's received from guns going off against it for over 70 years. It makes gun-mounting a bit of an effort, and natural, instinctive shooting more difficult.

I've always used full choke in my guns, and until a few years ago, only 7s for game, and often 7½s for pigeons. When I started shooting really high pheasants, it was with Charles Church, who had the Viri cartridge agency, and we used Supertrap 7s. Not much was then over 50 yards away, and you shot driven game in a fairly tight 'V' in front of you – thinking of your neighbours. Nowadays, too often, you see people shooting at birds over Guns two pegs away!

Pheasant shooting especially has changed over the last 10 years, and many shoots now show 'extreme' rather than just plain high pheasants. You need bigger shot than 7s for birds like that, so I now use 6s and even 5s for the really high stuff. Some people are using 4s and 3s, but if you need that heavy a cartridge I think you are getting into the realms of luck in killing a bird. There aren't many good enough to do it – but lots who think they are!

I'm not a fan of felt or fibre wad cartridges: I just don't think they pattern as well in a full-choke gun as a shotcup. It's all a matter of confidence, though, and, of course, in the old days, you could only buy felt, and I shot better then than now.

Nobody taught me to shoot. To me, it's all follow through. I can't understand these people who talk about 'lead', and ask me how far in front of something I was aiming! I say I couldn't tell them. I never consciously shoot in front of the target, though of course you have to, to hit it. I play it like a cricket shot – you swing through.

I now shoot a 20 bore

My mantra is 'speed of target; speed of swing'. You've got to read the line, too: whether he's drifting. The truly hard bird is a high, drifting one, where you've got to see the line, never mind what 'lead' is required by others. With age, I find it more difficult, and I sometimes miss with the first barrel because I haven't read the bird and swung properly, but I'll catch up with it with the second barrel. If he's flying straight: 'Come to daddy!' – tail, beak, bang... keep it going.

I have lost form in the past... for two or three shots! I generally know what I'm doing wrong. When I was younger, I didn't miss much. If it was a still day, and I was pigeon shooting, I'd kill everything. Of course I did miss – everyone does. Once, when I was a guest of Howard Bennett, I fell out with one fellow Gun. He turned up in an Aston Martin; he had all the kit – a Purdey, too, I seem to remember – but he wasn't much of a Shot. He asked me why I bothered to shoot, because I never missed! 'What's the point of doing it? It must get monotonous.' he enquired. I said whenever I was invited shooting, I tried to shoot as well as I could.

He kept jibing at me all day, and I got really annoyed.

I've always been able to concentrate, and everything else comes fairly naturally. Of course, footwork is vital. People say to me: 'Watch so-and-so: he's got a marvellous eye,' and I say: 'Look at his feet. He addresses his target, so the whole process is smooth.' Watch George [Digweed]: any bird that comes, he knows where he's going to kill it, and he does. For a man of his size, it's remarkable.

Now I have to do all my shooting sitting down, so I'm limited in the arc I can fire in. I have to position my body so that it's in the right place for where the majority of the birds are coming from. I can twist a little, and, being left-handed, I can swing through on my right, but birds well out of my left, I have to leave.

My problem now is what I call 'The Flinch': I just can't pull the trigger! Fred Cooper used to get it as well. It only happens occasionally – thank God – but it's like the Yips at golf. I never know when it's going to happen. It's not on any particular shot, and I try, and try, to pull the trigger, but my finger won't move. It's so frustrating – it never used to happen.

CHAPTER 17

FROM BEAUT TO CRUMPET

I've loved dogs all my life; I couldn't be without one. My father had a little cocker called Beaut, and she loved me. Much to my mother's irritation, Beaut would sneak up into my bedroom, and get under the blanket alongside me. Mother would say: 'Have you got Beaut?' and I'd say 'No, Mother.' But she'd lift the blanket, and there would be Beaut.

When Father was out ferreting with George Dunford, Beaut would often put up a hare, and off she'd go. She'd yap as she chased it, so we'd know where she was, but she was never as fast as the hare. George would say: 'Getting nearer, Guv'nor. Getting nearer!' A hare will often run round in a big circle, and when it came back, if it was within range, Father would shoot it – as long as it was sitting, not running – he didn't like to waste cartridges. Beaut would be along a minute later.

When I went to school as a boarder, I only got home on a Sunday, after chapel. The first thing I'd do is get my gun, and go off with Beaut. I often missed lunch, much to my parents' disapproval, but Beaut was expecting me, and off we'd go. I then had a Beaut of my own: a lovely liver and white springer, with a good pedigree. I decided to put her to dog, as there was good money in it. What a job I had with Mother when she had eight puppies. I wanted to keep them all. They would climb all over me, but she said I'd have to get rid of them. I put an advertisement in *Shooting Times* and got rid of several, but I had three dogs left.

Then I got a phone call from Lord Jellicoe, asking about the pups, and saying that he'd like to come down and see them. I was so excited, and cycled off to tell my cousins all about the call, and how Lord Jellicoe was coming down all the way from Lincolnshire next day to look at my pups. The following morning I groomed the pups till they were gleaming, and, answered the door at the appointed time, only to see my cousins standing there. 'We are Lord Jellicoe!' they said together. I could have killed them, but they had completely fooled me.

When I went off to Bridge Farm, I couldn't have a dog, but when I came home, I had a black lab from a puppy – a beautiful bitch called Sally, but, sadly, she was gun shy, and, despite my trying everything, I couldn't cure her of it, and she had to go.

I then had a lab called Brandy, from my friend Peter Osborne, who had a marvellous dog called Kim. Kim would find anything, and I told him that if he ever sired any pups, I'd have one. Brandy was the result: she was a sort of ginger

colour, and turned into the best pigeon dog I've ever had. She had quite a fiery temperament, though, and lived in my car – as almost all my dogs have done. It's their kennel. One day she bit a young girl who'd come to the house, and gone too close to the car. Jane said that Brandy would have to be put down, but I said: 'Over my dead body!' She'd lift her lip at anyone who came too close to the car.

She lived until she was 15. She had a lucky escape when we were wildfowling one night. Peter shot a mallard which was a swimmer, and Brandy went after it, but whenever she got close, it dived. It was getting quite dark, and we agreed that we would try to shoot the mallard again when it surfaced. We saw this shape on the water, and Peter fired…and then we realised it was Brandy, with the duck in her mouth. She was hit all down one side of her face, though luckily not in her eye, though her right ear was a bit shredded. Luckily, after a quick trip to the vet, she polished up all right!

She learned to turn a pigeon over that was lying on its back out in the decoy pattern. She'd seen me do it so many times, that she did it herself. She was a brilliant retriever: I remember shooting a pigeon, which I obviously hit in the head, stunning it, and it flew round and round, until it pitched in the field about 300 yards away. Brandy was watching it all the while, and I sent her for it, but, just as she got close, it took off. Brandy was underneath it as it fluttered across quite a busy road.

I was too far away to do anything. She leapt the fence, crossed the road, leapt the fence the other side, and picked the pigeon. Then she came back across the road – just as a car was coming. Luckily, the driver saw her, and skidded to a halt, before getting out of his car. He clearly didn't know what was going on, as I wasn't in sight. Back she came with the bird, and my heart was pumping!

She retrieved literally 1,000s of pigeons, until she got what I call 'pigeon dust'. She developed a cough, and eventually I had to take her to the vet who had a look, and found a growth in her throat. He said he'd never seen anything like it, and I asked whether it could have anything to do with the number of birds she'd retrieved. Pigeons dust regularly, and often you'll see a puff as they hit the ground. The vet came back to me, and said he thought I must be right. She was about 13 by now, and her breathing got so bad, that very reluctantly I had to have her put down.

I then had another couple of labs, one black, one yellow, both again called Beaut! Then Snipe, a springer; Whisky (who went blind through diabetes); Pickles and now I've got Crumpet. I've had springers for the last 30 years. They are great workers, and wonderful for pigeons. A labrador is really a peg dog, and I need a

Anticipation! Crumpet (left) and Boysie, who, as a stray, attached himself to us when on an Irish fishing trio, and was adopted by Bill and Julie Joyce hunter for pigeons. All my dogs have been a bit wild, and, one day, John Long said to me: 'Phil, what you ought to have is a shoot on the Isle of Wight... then at least you'd know where your dog was!'

Crumpet's been a great dog. She was the runt of the litter, but she caught my eye immediately. She was small, but she's been a great companion, and though she's eight now, you'd think she was a puppy. I wanted to call her 'Oi!', as I've forgotten how many times I've shouted 'Oi, you bloody dog!', but Jane said that I ought to call her what I had called Jane, when we were courting – my bit of crumpet! And the name stuck.

I had terriers, too, mainly as ratters. Freddie was the best, but he had a bad time when he cornered a badger, and got badly bitten on the face. He was covered in blood. I was with Fred Cooper, who had his humane killer with him, and, when the badger poked his head out, it was the last thing it did.

In the 1950s, I got into greyhound racing for a while. It was a disease with me, but stupid, as it was a racket run by crooks. I got so captivated by it, that I'd get myself out when playing cricket, just so I could go and see my dog run at Eastville in Bristol. It cost a lot of money, too: the dogs were expensive – I had six at one time – and the betting could get frightening. I got out after one last evening at Knowle, when I was persuaded to put £50 on a dog of Pat Mitchard's, and, luckily, it won by a short head at 4-1. I got a stack of white £5 notes, and I decided enough was enough.

CHAPTER 18

TODAY

I'm 84 now. Times have changed, and you've got to live with what happens today – you can't spend all your time hankering back to the old days. Rural life is very different, though: when I was young, everyone in the village were country people. Now a lot of them are town people who have moved out. They get too many of their views from TV programmes like *Springwatch*. Those presenters don't understand the realities of the countryside.

Losing Jane to cancer in 2007 was a terrible blow, but the support of my family, and my many good friends helped me to get over it. I'm very lucky, too, that my two sons are still putting up with me after all these years.

I'm usually up at 5.30 in the morning, and go out around the farm. I sit, and watch: there's always something to see... and something to shoot. I always have a rifle in the car, and there's often a crow, or a rat, or a squirrel. I also run tunnel traps, and they're checked daily: I'll usually get a couple of stoats a week in the spring. I got three foxes the other day, in five minutes: Whack! Whack! Whack! Very satisfying.

I still love pigeon shooting, but I'm happy now just to shoot a few on a flightline – so that Crumpet's got something to fetch – though sometimes they keep coming, and I make a good bag. My main worry now is falling over, as I find it difficult to get back on my feet.

I'll carry on shooting in my two syndicates – Tetton and Halse – as long as I can, and I'm fortunate still to have a few old friends who invite me. Last January, I had 18 days shooting! I just like to pick a good bird and kill it: something to remember at the end of the day, over a gin and tonic!

I always look forward to fishing at Chew, and up on the Spey, though it's getting to be hard work, now that I'm so unsteady. I was up there last May, and caught a salmon with my third cast. I didn't get another tug all week – that's salmon for you.

Most importantly, I'm still enjoying my sporting life, and, every day I think about how lucky I've been.

Sketched by grandson
Tom, September 2014

TRIBUTES

FROM HOWARD BENNETT:

An old friend once asked me quite seriously what I would like to do if I could have my life over again, and, with no hesitation, I replied: 'I'd like to be Philip Fussell!' He knew Philip well, and couldn't believe my response, saying that Philip had spent all his time doing what he wanted to do, playing sports, not doing much work, and having a good time. I said: 'I can't see much wrong with that!'

A lot of people are good at things, but they aren't necessarily nice people, and a lot are miserable beggars. Philip is just the best company you can get. The fun and laughter we've shared over the years – and all his friends would say the same.

FROM BOB BROWNING:

I've never seen anyone concentrate as Philip does when he's fishing: he's miles away. I can see him now – tongue out, eyes fixed, and in a world of his own. You could stand behind him – quite close – and he simply wouldn't be aware of you.

He had special eyesight, too. He could see fish follow the fly – fish that I couldn't see with polarised glasses on. That's why he found cricket easy, and why he's still such a good shot. He was the star turn in the old days. He rarely missed.

FROM SUSIE CHURCH:

When Charles reached 40, he decided he was going to take some time off – firstly for shooting, and then, for flying. So he organised his life to do just that: he was very good at analysing things, and he studied Philip very closely, and tried to copy him, and learn from him, as far as he could.

Charles was amazed by Fussell's whole demeanour, and the fact that he was such good fun: he wanted to be like him. He worked out that, when he was shooting, Fussell didn't really give the bird any lead the way most people seem to. He always started on the tail of the bird; quickly worked out the speed; and then gave what we called 'The Fussell flick' – a nice bit of acceleration at the end. But, if you watch him, his whole body is in harmony: his feet would automatically go in the right place, his body would swivel in the right way, and he'd look graceful, as all good shots do. He also has an amazing capacity for concentration: he could be chattering away to someone, but when it comes to taking a shot, then everything else is closed off, and he can totally focus, and have all the time in the world.

If Philip missed, and someone wiped his eye, it was a cause of much celebration – but it didn't happen every often, He just hardly ever missed a bird. I remember Jackie Stewart saying that when his concentration was at its peak – during a race – that time seemed to slow down, and he noticed everything that happened in slow motion. He would even see someone in the crowd putting up an umbrella, as he whizzed by at 150mph. I think Philip had this same capacity.

At the end of the drive, he can remember everything about it: exactly how all the shots happened, the cocks and hens, and where they fell – and where yours fell as well. He was always very encouraging to someone like me – a new girl in a very male dominated sport. It's changed a bit now, but then there were very few women who actually shot in the line.

It was all great fun then: the 'A-Team' were a raucous lot, and would gather and chat about their latest exploits – often with women. Now, when they meet up, it's to discuss their latest operations!

He's genuinely very loved. You could say he's lived a life of complete selfishness, doing all the things he loves – but nobody's resented it, as he's been so nice about it. He's such a tremendous sportsman, and an inspiration to others.

FROM RAY HILLYER:

Quite simply, he's always been my hero. He's 16 years older than me, and I've always looked up to him. A true countryman, he always gives the young good advice. He shoots so well, and he's that rare nice man, who never runs anybody down... and he's always good fun.

FROM DAVID HITCHINGS:

I was shooting with Philip once at Iwerne Minster in Dorset, where there are several very good drives. I had drawn the next peg to him, and, on one drive, simply stopped shooting to watch him in action. He was phenomenal.

He was such a stylish shot. I'm sure his cricketing background helped: his timing was immaculate. There were other people around then, who were as good as him on some days, but Philip was so consistent – always on form. I never saw him shoot badly.

FROM BILL JOYCE:

I don't think he found shooting hard. He was a natural, and he shot with some other great Guns. He made it look so easy. He's left-handed, and I've never seen a bad left-handed shot. I shoot a lot, but I don't think like him. I drive him to shoots, and, as we go, he'll be talking about birds, and what to think about, before you shoot it. Inexperienced Guns will treat every bird the same, but you have to really watch every bird, and see what it's doing. Then, you have to decide where you're going to shoot it, and get your feet in the right place. Philip did it all without apparent thought.

FROM BASIL KINCH:

I feel lucky to have Philip as a friend. He's a proper countryman, who knows it all, as he's done it all. He's a great host, and treats everyone the same, whoever they are – he's a real gentleman.

He's been an outstanding Shot: high or low; fur or feather, he shot them all equally well. He's great company, and has shot here at Halse for 20 odd years, and loves that one good bird – I still remember one hen pheasant he shot on my old Langford Down farm: it flew over the pylon lines, and had been missed by several other Guns. He killed it stone dead. He'd still remember it, too, and that's 35 years ago!

FROM NORMAN MARSHALL:

He's the most wonderful man you could ever want to meet, and his knowledge of the countryside is unbelievable. Every year now, when I invite him to shoot, Philip says he can't come, he's too old, and I tell him 'You've got to come; we'll come and get you if you don't!' He's always been the life and soul of the party: once at Bleasdale, after an excellent dinner, he and Lawrence Gardner demolished a bottle of brandy, but he was still first up the following morning.

FROM BOB MERRICK:

It's a privilege to have met and spent so much time with Philip. There's never been a better Shot, or a better ambassador for the sport of shooting. He mixes with everyone, and treats everybody exactly the same. He's great company, and knows how to enjoy himself. At 3am one morning, while staying at the Tufton Arms in Appleby when we were grouse shooting, I was woken by a naked Philip, who said: 'I can't find Mother (his name for Jane).' I reassured him that she was probably tucked up in bed at Shawford, as she hadn't come with us!

When I first bought Ballington in Wiltshire, I was new to shooting, and asked a friend to recommend someone who could help me improve the shoot. He suggested Philip, who came and looked round with me. He knew immediately what needed to be done, and made decisions on the spot, all of which turned out to be good ones. I particularly remember a wood with a release pen in it, which had a block of maize in its centre. Philip told me to get rid of it, saying: 'They can't have breakfast in bed; they've got to go and find it.'

He was very kind and considerate to the old keeper then there, John Yandle, and we all worked together to improve the shoot. Philip particularly enjoyed the smaller family days at Ballington, and seemed to have just as much fun when he was picking up with his unruly spaniel, Pickles.

FROM DAVID OLIVE:

Philip is the most natural Shot I've ever seen. There have been a lot of great Shots in the last 50 years, but their techniques have been awful. You'd never have taught anyone to shoot like that, but for some people it works. I've never seen anyone shoot as well at game as Philip. If one compares him, in his prime, to George Digweed, Philip was better. George's concentration is phenomenal, and desire to win outstanding, but Philip just didn't miss. If you were ever on a pheasant shoot in woodland, you could see where Philip was, as he didn't just hit the birds, he killed them stone dead, one after the other.

I remember watching him shoot pigeons one day near Sutton Scotney. There were lots of pigeons, and they were coming in sometimes 50 together. Not only would he almost always get two down, he'd always shoot the correct one first, and his timing was immaculate – second to none. And they weren't on the end of his barrels either, they were well out.

He has wonderful concentration, too: he once said to me: 'I've never once fired a shot in my life, without really meaning to hit what I was aiming at.' On a pheasant drive, you could see him, sitting on his shooting-stick, watching intently how the birds were flying.

He's also a gentleman Shot: there are some good Shots who are greedy with it. Philip isn't, and he'd never show up a neighbour, for example, by continually wiping his eye, as some do.

FROM ROBIN PARDOE:

He's always been the most sociable member of the syndicate. I was thrilled when I heard he wanted to join Tetton. He's a great asset, and a pleasure to shoot with. He's not greedy, but you don't want to be back gun behind him! I've never seen anyone – anyone! – to touch him in his pomp. You can always see the birds he's shot: they are DEAD. Their heads go back; he doesn't wound them, they just die. His technique is wonderful.

In the early days of the syndicate, there wasn't the emphasis on producing high birds that there is now, but Philip always wanted the most sporting birds. I think it was the first time he came to the shoot – as a guest of Reg Smith, I think – and we were doing a drive we called 'Over the Road'. The line was pegged above the road, but Philip asked if he could go down in the valley, the other side of the road. I had no problem with that, but thought 'Bloody idiot: he won't shoot anything down there!' He killed 13 pheasants that the front Guns had missed, and I then realised that pheasants could be killed much higher than we thought. From that day, we always stood below the road.

Tongue in cheek, he loves to mention that 'We public schoolboys must stick together!' but he has a great gift of getting on with everybody. It doesn't matter who he's with. The keepers, beaters and pickers-up all love him, and, of course, love his shooting ability. He's a real countryman, and he hates vermin with a passion, as I do; he also hates the fact that a lot of the so-called conservation organisations are anything but.

He's always been very careful with his cash – he's famous for it – and I was amazed when he wanted to join the syndicate, as he would have to pay out real money! One of his sayings is: 'Life's for living' – I'd add: '…as long as it doesn't cost Phil too much!'

FROM ANDY PUTTOCK:

He was phenomenal in his day. In my opinion – and others, too – he is the greatest gameshot the world has ever seen. I've seen him shoot for over 50 years. His fieldcraft was unbelievable. He always knew where the birds were likely to go: he was so aware. There wouldn't be much in it if he was measured against George Digweed.

I remember meeting Philip for the first time. It was at Buckland in Berkshire and I was asked to come by the keeper because he was short of beaters. He said to me: 'There's a Gun coming up from Somerset – he's been here three times already, and he hasn't missed one yet!'

Wherever he was, he would shine! He was known throughout the West Country – as good a gameshot as you would ever want to see. There was no-one to compare with him. To be a good shot, you have to be able to shoot every type of quarry – not just be known as a high pheasant shot, or great on grouse. He could shoot everything, and was so social with it: he'd shoot all day, and socialise all night.

FROM KEN RAINES:

Phil loved coming up here to shoot the partridges, and it wasn't often he didn't have a right and left – there was nothing he couldn't shoot. If you wanted some birds shot, he was the boy to do it. He came up here to shoot the pheasants. There weren't many, and they weren't very good ones, but he shot a lovely high hen, and, afterwards, he said to me: 'Surprising how one pheasant can make the day!' He just enjoyed being there.

FROM JEAN STEEDS:

He's the best, most loyal friend you could ever want. If I was ever in trouble, I'd go straight to Philip. I remember once when John chopped off two of his fingers in a farming accident; of course, it was in the middle of the rearing season, and Philip came over morning and evening every day for two weeks, to check on the broodies, until John had recovered.

FROM PETER STRATTON:

In all sports there are icons who stand out head and shoulders above the rest. In our small arena, Fussell stands out: his great skill with rod and gun coupled with a concentrational ability so intense that distraction was impossible.

It has been my privilege to have fished with him for over 40 years, during which time we've enjoyed together many memorable moments.

INDEX